THE
COMPLETE
WEATHER
RESOURCE

THE COMPLETE WEATHER RESOURCE

Volume 1:
Understanding Weather

Phillis Engelbert

AN IMPRINT OF GALE

DETROIT · NEW YORK · TORONTO · LONDON

THE COMPLETE WEATHER RESOURCE

by Phillis Engelbert

Staff

Jane Hoehner, *U·X·L Senior Editor*
Carol DeKane Nagel, *U·X·L Managing Editor*
Thomas L. Romig, *U·X·L Publisher*

Mary Beth Trimper, *Production Director*
Evi Seoud, *Assistant Production Manager*
Shanna P. Heilveil, *Production Assistant*

Cynthia Baldwin, *Product Design Manager*
Barbara J. Yarrow, *Graphic Services Supervisor*
Pamela A. E. Galbreath, *Cover and Page Designer*

Margaret Chamberlain, *Permissions Specialist (Pictures)*
Jeffrey Hermann, *Permissions Assistant*

Marco Di Vita, Graphix Group, *Typesetting*

Library of Congress Cataloging-in-Publication Data
Engelbert, Phillis.

The Complete Weather Resource / Phillis Engelbert.
    p. cm.
Includes biographical references and index.
Contents: v. 1. Understanding weather — v. 2. Weather phenomena
— v. 3. Forecasting & climate.
    ISBN 0-8103-9788-9 (vol. 1 : alk. paper). — ISBN 0-8103-9789-7
(vol. 2 : alk. paper). — ISBN 0-8103-9790-0 (vol. 3 : alk. paper).
    — ISBN 0-8103-9787-0 (set : alk. paper)
    1. Weather. 2. Climatology. 3. Meteorology.   I. Title.
QC981.E66 1997
551.5—dc21
    97-6930
    CIP

TM This book is printed on acid-free paper that meets the minimum requirements of American National Standard for Information Sciences—Permanence Paper for Printed Library Materials, ANSI Z39.48-1984.

Printed in the United States of America

10 9 8 7 6 5 4 3 2

TABLE OF CONTENTS

Table of Contents

READER'S GUIDE

The Complete Weather Resource presents under one title the most comprehensive survey of weather and weather-related topics to date, and it provides the clearest possible explanations for the many complex weather processes. The writing in *The Complete Weather Resource* is nontechnical and is geared to challenge, not overwhelm, students.

Volume 1, "Understanding Weather," focuses on basic atmospheric processes such as global and local winds, air pressure, heat and temperature, cloud formation, and front and storm formation.

"Weather Phenomena," Volume 2, offers in-depth discussions on precipitation, thunderstorms, tornadoes, hurricanes, temperature and precipitation extremes, and rainbows and other optical phenomena.

The third volume, "Forecasting and Climate," introduces the reader to several facets of these two topics. The "Forecasting" section provides information on state-of-the-art forecasting equipment and explains how to create forecasts using a backyard weather center. The "Climate" section describes climates of the world, changes in global climate throughout history, and reasons for climate change. Volume 3 concludes with a discussion on global warming, ozone depletion, and other environmental ills, as well as some steps that can be taken to protect the planet.

SCOPE AND FORMAT

The Complete Weather Resource is organized into chapters that are divided into topics and subtopics. The text is interspersed with boxes containing experiments, biographies, interesting weather facts, examples of extreme weather, and more. Approximately 140 photos, plus more than 65 original illustrations and charts, keep the volumes lively and entertaining. Additionally, *The Complete Weather Resource* features cross-references, a glossary (glossary words are bolded throughout the text), and a cumulative index in all three volumes that provides easy access to the topics discussed throughout *The Complete Weather Resource*.

ADVISORS

Chris Gleason
Science Teacher, Greenhills School
Ann Arbor, Michigan

Ann Novak
Science Teacher, Greenhills School
Ann Arbor, Michigan

DEDICATION

The author dedicates this work to her brother, Jon Engelbert, for the sunshine he brings to her life.

SPECIAL THANKS

Special thanks go to Jane Hoehner, Senior Editor at U•X•L, for masterfully coordinating every aspect of this project; to David Newton for verifying the scientific soundness of this writing; to Pete Caplan, Meteorologist at the National Weather Service's National Center for Environmental Prediction, for answering numerous questions; and to Dr. Richard Wood, Meteorologist, for checking facts in the final manuscript.

COMMENTS AND SUGGESTIONS

We welcome your comments on this work as well as your suggestions for topics to be featured in future editions of *The Complete Weather Resource*. Please write: Editors, *The Complete Weather Resource,* U•X•L, 835 Penobscot Bldg., Detroit, Michigan 48226-4094; call toll-free: 1-800-877-4253; or fax: 313-877-6348.

A

Absolute humidity: the amount of water vapor in the air, expressed as a ratio of the amount of water per unit of air.

Absolute zero: the temperature at which all motion ceases, -460°F (-273°C).

Accretion: the process by which a **hailstone** grows larger, by gradually accumulating cloud droplets as it travels through a cloud.

Acid fog: fog that is made more acidic by sulfuric and/or nitric acid in the air.

Acid rain: rain that is made more acidic by sulfuric and/or nitric acid in the air.

Adiabatic process: a process by which the temperature of a moving **air parcel** changes, even though no heat is exchanged between the air parcel and the surrounding air.

Advection fog: fog that forms when a warm, moist layer of air crosses over a cold surface.

Aerogenerator: an elevated windmill with very large blades.

Aerologist: someone who observes and gives reports of local atmospheric conditions.

Agricultural report: a specialized weather report, tailored to the needs of farmers, that includes current temperature, precipitation, and wind speed and direction, as well as frost warnings and predictions of temperature and precipitation for the days to come.

Air mass: a large quantity of air throughout which temperature and moisture content is fairly constant.

Air-mass thunderstorm: a relatively weak **thunderstorm** that forms within a single mass of warm, humid air.

Air-mass weather: unchanging weather conditions that result when a single **air mass** remains over a region for an extended period.

Air parcel: a small volume of air that has a consistent temperature and experiences minimal mixing with the surrounding air.

Air pollutant: any harmful substance that exists in the atmosphere at concentrations great enough to endanger the health of living organisms.

Air pressure: the pressure exerted by the weight of air over a given area of Earth's surface. Also called atmospheric pressure or barometric pressure.

Air stability: the temperature of the air at various heights, which determines whether an **air parcel** of a given temperature will rise, fall, or remain stationary.

Alberta Clipper: a dry, polar **air mass** that sweeps southward from Canada.

Altocumulus: clouds that looks like puffy masses and often appear in parallel rows or waves, that occupy an intermediate height in the **troposphere.**

Altostratus: nondescript, white, gray, or blue-gray, flat sheets of clouds that cover the entire sky and exist at an intermediate height in the **troposphere.**

Anabatic wind. *See* **Valley breeze**

Anemometer: an instrument used to measure wind speed, such as the **cup anemometer.**

Aneroid barometer: a type of **barometer** that consists of a vacuum-sealed metal capsule, within which a spring expands or contracts with changing **air pressure.**

Anticyclone: a weather system in which winds spiral clockwise, away from a high-pressure area.

Anvil: the flattened formation at the top of a mature **cumulonimbus** cloud.

Arctic climate: a **climate** type in which average temperatures remain below freezing, year-round, and the ground never thaws.

Arctic sea smoke: patchy, wispy **steam fog** that forms over unfrozen waters in arctic regions.

Atmospheric pressure. *See* **Air pressure**

Aurora: a bright, colorful display of light in the night sky, produced when charged particles from the sun enter Earth's atmosphere.

Avalanche: the cascading of some 100,000 tons of snow down a steep slope.

Aviation report: a specialized weather report, tailored to the needs of pilots, that provides information on the height of the clouds, visibility, and storm systems.

B

Backing wind: a wind that shifts direction, counterclockwise, with height.

Ball lightning: a mysterious form of **lightning** that is reported to look like a lighted sphere, ranging from .4 to 40 inches (1 to 100 centimeters) in diameter.

Banner cloud: a banner-shaped cloud that forms at a mountain's peak and drapes down over the **leeward slope.**

Barchan dune: a **sand dune** that, when viewed from above, resembles a crescent moon, with the tips of the crescent pointing downwind. Also called barchane dune, barkhan dune, or crescentic dune.

Barograph: an **aneroid barometer** that records changes in **air pressure** over time on a rotating drum.

Barometer: an instrument used to measure **air pressure.**

Barometric pressure. *See* **Air pressure**

Bead lightning: lightning that resembles a string of beads, that may be the result of the fragmentation of an **ionized channel.**

Blizzard: the most severe type of winter storm, characterized by winds of 35 mph (56 kph) or greater, large quantities of snow, and temperatures of 20°F (-6°C) or lower.

Blocking high. *See* **Blocking system**

Blocking low. *See* **Blocking system**

Blocking system: a whirling **air mass** containing either a high-pressure system (a blocking high) or a low-pressure system (a blocking low), that gets cut off from the main flow of **upper-air westerlies.**

Blowing snow: snow that has been lifted off the surface by the wind and blown about in the air.

Bolide: a large, rocky body from space, such as an asteroid or comet.

Bolide winter: a theoretical consequence of Earth being struck by a **bolide,** in which virtually all sunlight is blocked out by a thick dust cloud for a period of several months.

Buttes: steep, rocky hills of the American West.

C

Carbon dating: a technique, similar to **radioactive dating,** that uses an analysis of radioactive carbon to determine the age of rocks.

Carcinogens: cancer-causing agents.

Celsius scale: the temperature scale on which fresh water freezes at 0 degrees and boils at 100 degrees. To convert from Celsius to **Fahrenheit,** multiply degrees Celsius by 1.8, then add 32.

Cenozoic Era: the historical period from 65 million years ago to the present.

Chaos Theory: the theory that the weather, by its very nature, is unpredictable. Every time one atmospheric variable (such as heat, air pressure, or water) changes, every other variable also changes—but in ways that are out of proportion with the first variable's change.

Chinook: a dry, warm **katabatic wind** that blows down the eastern side of the Rocky Mountains, from New Mexico to Canada, in winter or early spring.

Chinook wall cloud: a solid bank of wispy, white clouds that appears over the eastern edge of the Rockies in advance of a **chinook.**

Cirriform: a wispy, feathery fair-weather cloud formation that exists at high levels of the **troposphere.**

Cirrocumulus: high, small, white, rounded, and puffy clouds that occur individually or in patterns resembling rippled waves, at high levels of the **troposphere.**

Cirrostratus: clouds that cover all or part of the sky, at high levels of the **troposphere,** in a sheet thin enough for the sun or moon to be clearly visible.

Cirrus: clouds at high levels of the **troposphere,** created by wind-blown ice crystals, that are so thin as to be nearly transparent.

Cirrus spissatus: tightly packed, icy **cirrus** cloud formations at the top of a **vertical cloud** that are dense enough to block out the sun.

Climate: the weather experienced by a given location, averaged over several decades.

Cloud-to-air lightning: lightning that travels between oppositely charged areas of a cloud and the surrounding air.

Cloud-to-cloud lightning: lightning that occurs within a single cloud or between two clouds.

Cloud-to-ground lightning: lightning that travels between a cloud and the ground.

Cloudburst: The heaviest type of **shower,** in which rain falls at a rate of 4 inches (10 centimeters) or more per hour.

Coalescence: the process by which an ice crystal grows larger. The ice crystal collides, and sticks together, with water droplets as the ice crystal travels down through a cloud.

Coastal flood: a **flood** that occurs along the coasts of a lake or ocean.

Cold cloud: a cloud within which ice crystals coexist with **supercooled water** droplets.

Cold fog. *See* **Freezing fog**

Cold front: the line behind which a cold **air mass** is advancing, and in front of which a warm air mass is retreating.

Cold occlusion: the most common type of **occluded front,** in which a cold **air mass** overtakes a warm air mass.

Compressional heating. *See* **Compressional warming**

Compressional warming: an **adiabatic process** by which an **air parcel** warms as it descends. The descending parcel is compressed by the increasing pressure of the surrounding air, which leads to a greater number of collisions between molecules. Also called compressional heating.

Condensation: the process by which water changes from a gas to a liquid.

Condensation nucleus: a tiny solid particle around which **condensation** of water vapor occurs.

Conduction: the transfer of heat from a fast-moving, warm molecule to a slow-moving, cold molecule.

Conservation of angular momentum: the principle that states that as the radius of a spinning object decreases, its speed increases, and vice versa.

Continental drift: the theory that over the last 200 to 250 million years, forces deep within Earth's core have caused a single huge continent to break apart and drift around the globe.

Contrails: cirrus-like markings in the sky, created by aircraft flying at 16,500 feet (5 kilometers) or higher. "Contrails" is an abbreviation for "condensation trails."

Convection: the upward motion of an **air mass** or **air parcel** that has been heated.

Convective cell: a unit within a **thunderstorm cloud** that contains **updraft**s and **downdraft**s.

Conventional radar: an instrument that detects the location, movement, and intensity of precipitation, and gives indications about the type of precipitation. It operates by emitting microwaves, which are reflected by precipitation. Also called radar.

Convergence: The movement of air inward, toward a central point.

Coriolis effect: the apparent curvature of large-scale winds, ocean currents, and anything else that moves freely across Earth, due to the rotation of Earth about its axis.

Corona: a circle of light centered on the moon or sun that is usually bounded by a colorful ring or set of rings.

Cosmic rays: invisible, high-energy particles that bombard Earth from space.

Crepuscular rays: bright beams of light that radiate from the sun and stretch across the sky.

Critical angle: the angle at which sunlight must strike the back of the raindrop, in order to be reflected back to the front of the drop.

Cumuliform: a puffy, heaped-up cloud formation.

Cumulonimbus: tall, dark, ominous-looking clouds that produce **thunderstorm**s. Also called thunderstorm clouds.

Cumulonimbus incus: a fully developed **cumulonimbus** cloud, the top of which extends to the top, or beyond the top, of the **troposphere.**

Cumulus: clouds that look like white or light-gray cotton puff-balls of various shapes.

Cumulus congestus: a tall **cumulus** cloud that is shaped like a head of cauliflower.

Cumulus humilis: the smallest species of **cumulus** cloud, which looks like small tufts of cotton.

Cumulus mediocris: a **cumulus** cloud of medium height with a lumpy top.

Cumulus stage: the initial stage of **thunderstorm** development, during which **cumulus** clouds undergo dramatic vertical growth. Also called developing stage.

Cup anemometer: an instrument used to measure wind speed. It consists of three or four cups positioned on their sides, connected by horizontal spokes to a cap that rotates freely on a pole.

Cyclogenesis: the process by which an **extratropical cyclone** is formed.

Cyclone: 1. a weather system in which winds spiral counterclockwise, in toward a low-pressure area. Also called storm. 2. the name for a **hurricane** that forms over the Indian Ocean.

D

Dart leaders: The series of dim **lightning** strokes that occur immediately after the original lightning stroke, that serve to discharge the remaining buildup of electrons near the base of the cloud.

Decay stage: the final stage of **tornado** development during which the tornado's funnel narrows, twists and turns, fragments, and dissipates.

De-icing: the process of spraying the wings of an aircraft with antifreeze before take-off, to prevent ice from accumulating on the wings.

Dendrite: a **sector plate** that has accumulated moisture and developed feathery branches on its arms. A dendrite is the most distinctive and most common type of **snowflake.**

Dendrochronology: the study of the annual growth of rings of trees.

Deposition: the process by which water changes directly from a gas to a solid, without first going through the liquid phase.

Deposition nuclei: tiny, solid particles suspended on clouds onto which water vapor molecules directly freeze, by the process of **deposition.**

Derecho: a destructive, straight-line wind, that travels faster than 58 mph (93 kph) and has a path of damage at least 280 miles (450 kilometers) long. Also called plow wind.

Desert climate: the world's driest **climate** type, with less than 10 inches (25 centimeters) of rainfall annually.

Desert pavement: hard, flat, dry ground and gravel that remains after all sand and dust has been eroded from a surface.

Developing stage. *See* **Cumulus stage**

Dew: clumps of water molecules that have condensed on a cold surface.

Dew point: the temperature at which a given parcel of air reaches its **saturation point** and can no longer hold water in the vapor state.

Diamond dust. *See* **Ice fog**

Diffraction: the slight bending of sunlight or moonlight around water droplets or other tiny particles.

Dispersion: the selective **refraction** of light that results in the separation of light into the spectrum of colors.

Dissipating stage: the final stage of a **thunderstorm,** during which the rain becomes light, the wind weakens, and the thunderstorm cloud begins to **evaporate.**

Divergence: the movement of air outward, away from a central point.

The Doctor: a special name given to the **sea breeze** in some tropical areas, because it brings relief from the oppressive heat.

Doldrums: the cloudy, rainy zone near the equator where the **trade winds** coming from north and south meet and nearly cancel each other out.

Doppler radar: a sophisticated type of radar that relies on the Doppler effect—the change in frequency of waves emitted from a moving source—to determine wind speed and direction, as well as the direction in which precipitation is moving.

Downburst: an extremely strong, localized **downdraft** beneath a **thunderstorm,** that spreads horizontally when it hits the ground, destroying objects in its path.

Downdraft: a downward blast of air from a **thunderstorm cloud**, felt at the surface as a cool gust.

Drifting snow: loose snow that has been swept into large piles, or "drifts," by strong winds.

Drizzle: precipitation formed by raindrops between .008 inches and .02 inches in diameter.

Dropwindsonde: a device, similar to a **radiosonde,** that is released by an aircraft and transmits atmospheric measurements to a radio receiver.

Drought: an extended period of abnormal dryness.

Dry adiabatic lapse rate: the constant rate at which the temperature of an unsaturated **air parcel** changes as it ascends or descends through the atmosphere. Specifically, air cools by 5.5°F for every 1,000 feet it ascends and warms by 5.5°F for every 1,000 feet it descends.

Dry-bulb thermometer. *See* **Thermometer**

Dry tongue: a layer of cold, dry, air that exists at an altitude of 10,000 feet (3,048 meters) and is necessary for the formation of a **supercell storm.**

Dust Bowl: the popular name for the approximately 150,000 square-mile-area (400,000-square-kilometer-area) in the South Great Plains region of the United States, characterized by low annual rainfall, a shallow layer of topsoil and high winds.

Dust devil: a spinning **vortex** of sand and dust that is usually harmless but may grow quite large. Also called a whirlwind.

Dust-whirl stage: the first stage in the formation of a **tornado,** marked by the emergence of a short **funnel cloud** and the swirling of debris on the ground.

E

Eccentricity: the alternating change in shape of Earth's orbit between a circle and an ellipse.

Eddies: small **air parcel**s that flow in a pattern that is different than the general air flow.

Ekman Spiral: the changing direction of the flow of ocean water along a vertical gradient.

El Niño: the annual, brief period during which the normally cold waters off the coast of Peru are made warmer by the arrival of warm waters from the equatorial region.

El Niño/Southern Oscillation (ENSO): a period during which a **major El Niño event** and a **Southern Oscillation** both occur. These two phenomena are connected because the warming of the waters off the coast of Peru lowers the **air pressure** in the eastern Pacific. As a result, the air pressure in the western Pacific rises.

Electromagnetic radiation: radiation that transmits energy through the interaction of electricity and magnetism.

Electromagnetic spectrum: the array of **electromagnetic radiation,** which includes radio waves, infrared radiation, visible light, ultraviolet radiation, X-rays, and gamma rays.

Enhanced greenhouse effect. *See* **Global warming**

Ensemble forecasting: A forecasting method takes into account the predictability of the behavior of atmosphere at the time a forecast is made.

Entrainment: the process by which cool, **unsaturated air** next to a **thunderstorm cloud** gets pulled into the cloud during the **mature stage** of a thunderstorm.

Equinoxes: the days marking the start of spring and fall and the two days of the year in which day and night are most similar in length.

Evaporation: the process by which water changes from a liquid to a gas.

Evaporation fog: fog that is formed when water vapor evaporates into cool air and brings the air to its **saturation point.**

Exosphere: the outermost layer of Earth's atmosphere, starting about 250 miles (400 kilometers) above ground, in which molecules of gas break down into atoms and, due to the lack of gravity, escape into space.

Expansional cooling: an **adiabatic process** by which an **air parcel** cools as it rises. The cooling is due to decreasing **air pressure** with altitude, which allows the air parcel to expand and leads to a smaller number of collisions between molecules.

Extratropical cyclone: a storm system that forms outside of the tropics and involves contrasting warm and cold **air mass**es.

Eye: the calm circle of low-pressure that exists at the center of a **hurricane.**

Eye wall: the region of a **hurricane** immediately surrounding the **eye,** and the strongest part of the storm. The eye wall is a loop of **thunderstorm cloud**s that produce torrential rains and forceful winds.

F

Fahrenheit scale: the temperature scale on which fresh water freezes at 32 degrees and boils at 212 degrees. To convert from Fahrenheit to **Celsius,** subtract 32 from degrees Fahrenheit, then divide by 1.8.

Fair-weather waterspout: a relatively harmless **waterspout** that forms over water and arises either in conjunction with, or independently of, a **severe thunderstorm.** Also called non-tornadic waterspout.

Fall streaks: ice crystals that fall from a cloud, **sublimate** into dry air, and never reach the ground.

Fata Morgana: a special type of **superior mirage** that takes the form of spectacular castles, buildings, or cliffs, rising above cold land or water.

Ferrel cell: an atmospheric cell through which **westerlies** and **upper-air westerlies** circulate. Air rises at 60 degrees latitude and sinks at 30 degrees latitude, North and South.

Fetch: the distance over water that the wind blows, which is used to calculate the height of waves.

Flash flood: a sudden, intense, localized flooding caused by persistent, heavy rainfall or the failure of a levee or dam.

Flood: the inundation of normally dry land with water.

Flurries: the lightest form of snowfall, which is brief and intermittent and results in little accumulation

Foehn: a warm, dry **katabatic wind** similar to the **chinook** that flows down from the Alps onto the plains of Austria and Germany.

Fog: a cloud that forms near or on the ground.

Fog stratus: a layer of **fog** that hovers a short distance above ground, without touching the ground. Also called **high fog.**

Forked lightning: lightning that results when a **return stroke** originates from two different places on the ground at once.

Freezing drizzle: drizzle comprised of **supercooled water** that freezes on contact with a cold surface.

Freezing fog: fog comprised of **supercooled water** droplets that freeze on contact with a cold surface. Also called cold fog.

Freezing nucleus: a tiny particle of ice or other solid onto which **supercooled water** droplets can freeze.

Freezing rain: rain comprised of **supercooled water** that freezes on contact with a cold surface.

Front: the dividing line between two **air mass**es.

Frontal fog: a type of **evaporation fog** that forms when a layer of warm air rises over a shallow layer of colder surface air. Also called precipitation fog.

Frontal system: a weather pattern that accompanies an advancing **front.**

Frontal thunderstorm: a **thunderstorm** that forms along the edge of a **front.**

Frontal uplift: the upward motion of a warm **air mass** caused by an advancing cold air mass.

Frost: ice that forms on a cold surface when the air directly above the surface reaches the **frost point.**

Frost point: the temperature at which a given **air parcel** reaches its **saturation point** and thus can no longer hold water in the vapor state, provided that the temperature is below freezing.

Frostbite: the freezing of the skin.

Fujita Intensity Scale: a scale that measures **tornado** intensity, based on wind speed and the damage created. Also called Fujita-Pearson Scale or Fujita Scale.

Funnel cloud: a cone-shaped **tornado** that hangs well below the base of a **thunderstorm cloud.**

G

Geostationary satellite: a **weather satellite** that remains "parked" above a given point on the equator, traveling at the same speed as Earth's rotation about 22,300 miles (35,900 kilometers) above the surface.

Glaze: a layer of clear, smooth ice on a cold surface formed when **supercooled water** strikes the surface and spreads out.

Global warming: the theory that average temperatures around the world have begun to rise, and will continue to rise, due to an increase of certain gases, called **greenhouse gases,** in the atmosphere. Also called enhanced greenhouse effect.

Global water budget: the balance of the volume of water coming and going between the oceans, atmosphere, and continental landmasses.

Glory: a set of colored rings that appears on the top surface of a cloud, directly beneath the observer. A glory is formed by the interaction of sunlight with tiny cloud droplets and is most often viewed from an airplane.

Graupel. *See* **Snow pellets**

Green flash: a very brief flash of green light that appears near the top edge of a rising or setting sun.

Greenhouse effect: the warming of Earth due to the presence of **greenhouse gases,** which trap upward-radiating heat and return it to Earth's surface.

Greenhouse gases: gases that trap heat in the atmosphere. The most abundant greenhouse gases are water vapor and carbon dioxide. Others include methane, nitrous oxide, and chlorofluorocarbons.

Ground blizzard: the drifting and blowing of snow that occurs after a snowfall has ended.

Ground fog: a very shallow layer of **radiation fog** that exists just above the ground.

Gust front: the dividing line between cold **downdraft**s and warm air at the surface, characterized by strong, cold, shifting winds.

Gyres: large, circular patterns of **ocean currents.**

H

Haboob: a tumbling black wall of sand that has been stirred up by cold **downdraft**s along the leading edge of a **thunderstorm** or **cold front,** that occurs in north-central Africa and, rarely, in the southwestern United States.

Hadley cell: an atmospheric cell through which **trade winds** circulate. Air rises at the equator and sinks at 30 degrees latitude, North and South.

Hail: precipitation comprised of **hailstone**s.

Hailstone: frozen **precipitation** that is either round or has a jagged surface, is either totally or partially transparent, and ranges in size from that of a pea to that of a softball.

Hair hygrometer: an instrument that measures **relative humidity.** It uses hairs (human or horse), which grow longer and shorter in response to changing humidity.

Halo: a thin ring of light that appears around the sun or the moon, caused by the **refraction** of light by ice crystals.

Haze: the uniform, milky white appearance of the sky that results when humidity is high and there are a large number of particles in the air.

Heat burst: a sudden, short-lived, dramatic warming of the air that is produced in the wake of a dissipating **thunderstorm.**

Heat cramps: muscle cramps or spasms, usually afflicting the abdomen or legs, caused by exercising in hot weather.

Heat equator: the warmest part of the equatorial zone, which lies most directly beneath the sun. Also called intertropical convergence zone (ITCZ).

Heat exhaustion: a form of mild shock that results when fluid and salt are lost through heavy perspiration.

Heat lightning: lightning from a storm that is too far away for its accompanying **thunder** to be heard.

Heat stroke: a life-threatening condition that sets in when **heat exhaustion** is left untreated and the body has exhausted its efforts to cool itself. Also called sunstroke.

Heat syncope: fainting that is the result of a rapid drop in blood pressure, that sometimes occurs while exercising in hot weather.

Heat wave: an extended period of high heat and humidity.

Heating-degree-days: the number of degrees difference between the day's mean temperature and an arbitrarily selected temperature at which most people set their thermostats. The number of heating-degree-days in a season is an indicator of how much heating fuel has been consumed.

Heavy rain: precipitation that falls at a rate greater than .3 inches (.76 centimeters) per hour.

Heavy snow: snowfall that reduces visibility to .31 miles (.5 kilometers) and yields, on average, 4 inches (10 centimeters) or more in a twelve-hour period or 6 inches (15 centimeters) or more in a twenty-four-hour period.

High fog. *See* **Fog stratus**

Highland climate. *See* **Mountain climate**

Hoar frost: frost that is formed by the process of **sublimation.** Also called true frost.

Hollow-column: a **snowflake** in the shape of a long, six-sided column.

Holocene epoch: the second part of the **Cenozoic Era,** from 10,000 years ago to the present.

Horse latitudes: a high-pressure belt that exists at around 30 degrees latitude, North and South, where air from the equatorial region descends and brings clear skies.

Humid subtropical climate: a **climate** type that has hot, muggy summers and mild, wet winters.

Humiture index: an index that combines temperature and **relative humidity** to determine how hot it actually feels and, consequently, how stressful outdoor activity will be. Also called temperature-humidity index or heat index.

Hurricane: the most intense form of **tropical cyclone.** A hurricane is a storm made up of a series of tightly coiled bands of **thunderstorm cloud**s, with a well-defined pattern of rotating winds and maximum sustained winds greater than 74 mph (119 kph).

Hydrologic cycle. *See* **Water cycle**

Hygrometer. *See* **Psychrometer**

Hypothermia: a condition characterized by a drop in core body temperature from the normal 98.6°F to below 95°F.

I

Ice age: a period during which significant portions of Earth's surface were covered with ice.

Ice fog: fog comprised of ice crystals that forms at temperatures below -22°F (-30°C). Also called diamond dust.

Ice pellets: Frozen raindrops formed by **precipitation** that first pass through a warm layer of air and melt, after which they enter a layer of freezing air and re-freeze.

Ice storm: a heavy downpour of **freezing rain** that deposits a layer of **glaze** more than an inch thick on solid objects it encounters.

Inferior mirage: a **mirage** that appears as an inverted, lowered image of a distant object. It forms in hot weather.

Instrument shelter: a ventilated wooden box on legs that is used to store and protect weather instruments outdoors. Also called a Stevenson screen or weather shack.

Insulator: a substance through which electricity does not readily flow.

Interglacial period: a relatively warm period that exists between two **ice ages**.

International weather symbols: the internationally accepted set of symbols used by meteorologists to describe many atmospheric conditions.

Intertropical convergence zone (ITCZ). *See* **Heat equator**

Inversion: an increase in air temperature with height.

Ionized: the condition of an object that has a positive or negative electrical charge.

Ionized channel: the path between a cloud and the ground, through which electrons flow, that is created when the **return stroke** of **lightning** contacts the **stepped leader.**

Ionosphere: the region of upper **mesosphere** and lower **thermosphere** in which molecules become **ionized** by X-rays and ultraviolet rays that exist in solar radiation.

Iridescence: an irregular patch of colored light on a cloud.

Isobar: an imaginary line that connects areas of equal **air pressure** that have undergone a **reduction to sea level.**

Isotherm: an imaginary line connecting areas of similar temperature.

J

Jet streams: narrow bands of fast winds that zip through the top of the **troposphere** in a west-to-east direction at speeds between 80 and 190 mph (128 and 305 kph).

K

Katabatic wind: a downhill wind that is considerably stronger than a **mountain breeze.**

Kelvin-Helmholtz clouds: thin clouds produced by **wind shear,** that look like a series of breaking ocean waves, in the upper levels of the **troposphere.**

Kinetic energy: the energy of motion.

L

Lake breeze: a **sea breeze**-type wind that can be felt on the edge of a large lake.

Lake-effect snow: a heavy snow that falls on the land downwind of the Great Lakes.

Land breeze: the gentle wind that blows from the shore to the water, due to differences in **air pressure** above each surface, at night.

Landfall: the passage of a **hurricane** from the ocean onto land.

Latent heat: the energy that is either absorbed by or released by a substance as it undergoes a phase change.

Latitude: an imaginary line encircling Earth, parallel to the equator, that tell one's position North or South on the globe.

Leeward slope: the eastward side of the mountain, on which cold air descends, producing dry conditions.

Lenticular cloud: a disc-shaped cloud that forms downwind of a mountain and remains in the sky for an extended period of time.

Lightning: a short-lived, bright flash of light during a **thunderstorm** that is produced by a 100-million-volt electrical discharge in the atmosphere.

Lightning rod: a metal pole that is attached to the tallest point of a building and connected, by an insulated conducting cable, to a metal rod buried deep the ground.

Local winds. *See* **Mesoscale winds.**

Longitude: an imaginary line encircling Earth, perpendicular to the equator, that tell one's position East or West on the globe.

M

Macroburst: a **downburst** that creates a path of destruction on the surface greater than 2.5 miles (4 kilometers) wide. The winds of a macroburst travel at around 130 mph (210 kph) and last up to thirty minutes.

Major El Niño event: a one- or two-year-long period during which the ocean waters off the coast of Peru remain warm. This prolonged warming, which has a variety of negative ecological consequences, occurs once every three to seven years.

Mammatus: round, pouch-like cloud formations that appear in clusters and hang from the underside of a larger cloud.

Marine climate: a coastal **climate** type that is characterized by cool summers, mild winters, and low clouds. **Fog** and **drizzle** are present for much of the year.

Marine forecast: a specialized weather forecast, of interest to coastal residents and mariners, that gives projections of the times of high and low tide, wave height, wind speed and direction, and visibility.

Mature stage: 1. the stage of **thunderstorm** development that begins when the first drops of rain reach the ground and is characterized by heavy rain, strong winds, **lightning,** and sometimes **hail** and **tornado**es. 2. the stage of tornado development during which the funnel reaches all the way to the ground and the tornado is at its most destructive.

Maunder minimum: the stretch of years from 1645 to 1715, during which **sunspot** activity was at a very low level.

Maximum and minimum thermometers: thermometers that record the highest and lowest temperatures during an observation period.

Mediterranean climate: a **climate** type characterized by dry summers and rainy, mild winters.

Melting zone: the atmospheric height at which the air becomes warm enough for falling snow to turn to rain.

Meltwater equivalent: the water content of snow.

Mercurial barometer: a type of **barometer** that relies on changes in a column of mercury to measure **air pressure.**

Mesocyclone: a region of rotating **updraft**s created by **wind shear** within a **supercell storm,** that may be a precursor to a **tornado.**

Mesoscale convective complex (MCC): a group of **thunderstorm**s that forms a nearly circular pattern over an area that is about a thousand times the size of an individual thunderstorm.

Mesoscale winds: winds that blow across areas of the surface ranging from a few miles to a hundred miles in width. Also known as **local winds** or **regional winds.**

Mesosphere: the middle layer of Earth's atmosphere, that exists between 40 and 50 miles (65 and 80 kilometers) above ground.

Mesozoic Era: the historical period from 225 million years ago to 65 million years ago, best known as the age of the dinosaurs.

Meteorology: the scientific study of the atmosphere and atmospheric processes, namely weather and climate.

Microburst: a very intense **downburst,** with winds that may exceed 167 mph (270 kph), that creates a path of destruction on the surface from several hundred yards wide to 2.5 miles (4 kilometers) wide.

Middle latitudes: the regions of the world that lie between the latitudes of 30 degrees and 60 degrees, North and South. Also called temperate regions.

Milankovitch theory: the theory stating that there are three types of variations in Earth's orbit that, taken together, can be linked with warm and cold periods throughout history. These variations include: the shape of Earth's orbit, the direction of tilt of its axis, and the degree of tilt of its axis.

Mirage: an optical illusion in which an object appears in a position that differs from its true position or in which a nonexistent object, such as a body of water, appears.

Mist: condensation that occurs in the low-lying air, in which visibility is greater than 1 kilometer.

Moist adiabatic lapse rate: the variable rate at which the temperature of a saturated **air parcel** changes as it ascends or descends through the atmosphere.

Monsoon climate: a **climate** type that is warm year-round with very rainy summers and relatively dry winters.

Moon dogs: patches of light, similar to **sundogs,** seen around a very bright, full moon.

Mountain breeze: a gentle downhill wind that forms at night as cold, dense, surface air travels down a mountainside and sinks into the valley. Also called gravity wind or drainage wind.

Mountain climate: the series of **climate** types that are found at various points ascending a mountainside. The range climate types results because temperature decreases with altitude. Also called highland climate.

Mountain-wave clouds: a class of clouds, including **lenticular cloud**s and **banner cloud**s, that are generated when moist wind crosses over a mountain range.

Multicell storm: a **thunderstorm** that contains several **convective cell**s.

Multi-vortex tornado: a **tornado** in which the **vortex** divides into several smaller vortices called **suction vortices.**

N

NEXRAD: Acronym for Next Generation Weather Radar, the network of 156 high-powered **Doppler radar** units which cover the continental United States, Alaska, Hawaii, Guam, and Korea.

Nimbostratus: dark gray, wet-looking layers of clouds that cover all or a large part of the sky, at low levels of the **troposphere.**

Nimbus: a dark, rain-producing cloud formation.

Nor'easter: a strong, northeasterly wind that brings cold air, often accompanied by heavy rain, snow, or sleet, to the coastal areas of New England and the mid-Atlantic states. Also called northeaster.

Northern Hemisphere: the half of Earth that lies north of the equator.

Numerical forecasting: the use of mathematical equations, performed by computers, to predict the weather.

O

Obliquity: the angle of the tilt of Earth's axis in relation to the plane of its orbit.

Occluded front: a **front** formed by the interaction of three **air mass**es: one cold, one cool, and one warm. The result is a multi-tiered air system, with cold air wedged on the bottom, cool air resting partially on top of the cold air, and warm air on the very top.

Ocean currents: the major routes through which ocean water is circulated around the globe.

Organized convection theory: the most widely accepted model of how a **hurricane** forms. It includes the formation of large **thunderstorm cloud**s, the transformation of a low-pressure area aloft into a high-pressure area (with a resultant low-pressure area at the surface), and the successive formation of spiraling bands of thunderstorms.

Organizing stage: the second stage of **tornado** formation, during which the **funnel cloud** extends part way to the ground and increases in strength.

Orographic lifting: the upward motion of warm air that occurs when a warm **air mass** travels up the side of a mountain.

Orographic thunderstorm: a type of **air-mass** thunderstorm that's initiated by the flow of warm air up a mountainside. Also called mountain thunderstorm.

Overshooting: the condition in which powerful **updraft**s rise above the **troposphere** and penetrate the **stratosphere.**

Ozone hole: the region above Antarctica in which the ozone layer virtually disappears at the end of each winter.

Ozone layer: the layer of Earth's atmosphere, between 25 and 40 miles (40 and 65 kilometers) above ground, that filters out the sun's harmful rays. It consists of ozone, which is a form of oxygen that has three atoms per molecule.

P

Paleoclimatologist: a scientist who studies **climate**s of the past.

Paleozoic Era: the historical period from 570 million years ago to 225 million years ago.

Particulate matter: air pollutants in the form of tiny solid or liquid particles, that creates the most visible type of air pollution.

Permafrost: a layer of subterranean soil that remains frozen year-round.

Photochemical smog: a hazy layer of surface ozone that sometimes appears brown. It is produced when pollutants that are released by car exhaust fumes react with strong sunlight.

Photovoltaic cell: an instrument that converts sunlight to electricity.

Pileus: smooth cloud formations that are found at the top of **cumulus congestus** or **cumulonimbus** clouds. Also called cap clouds.

Polar cell: an atmospheric cell that caps each pole, extending to 60 degrees latitude North and South. Relatively warm **westerlies** are carried poleward, and cold **polar easterlies** are carried equatorward, through each polar cell.

Polar climate: a **climate** type that covers the extreme northern and southern portions of Earth. It encompasses both **tundra climate** and **arctic climate.**

Polar easterlies: Cold, global winds that travel across the polar regions, from the northeast to the southwest in the **Northern Hemisphere** and from the southeast to the northwest in the **Southern Hemisphere.**

Polar fronts: The belts that encircle Earth at about 60 degrees latitude North and South, where the **westerlies** encounter **polar easterlies.**

Polar-orbiting satellite: a **weather satellite** that travels in a north-south path, crossing over both poles just 500 to 625 miles (800 to 1,000 kilometers) above Earth's surface.

Pre-frontal squall line: a **squall line** that forms some 100 to 200 miles (160 to 320 kilometers) ahead of a **cold front.**

Pre-Holocene epoch: the early part of the **Cenozoic Era,** from 65 million years ago to 10,000 years ago.

Precambrian Era: the historical period beginning with the formation of Earth, around 4.6 billion years ago, and ending 570 million years ago.

Precession of the equinoxes: the reversal of the **season**s every 13,000 years. This occurs because Earth spins about its axis like a top in slow motion and wobbles its way through one complete revolution every 26,000 years.

Precipitation: water particles that originate in the atmosphere (usually referring to water particles that form in clouds) and fall to the ground.

Precipitation fog. *See* **Frontal fog**

Pressure gradient: the rate at which **air pressure** decreases with horizontal distance.

Pressure gradient force (PGF): the force that causes winds to blow from an area of high pressure to an area of low pressure, that is proportional to the **pressure gradient.**

Prevailing winds: the winds blowing in the direction that's observed most often during a given time period.

Primary air pollutant: an **air pollutant** that is emitted directly into the air.

Psychrometer: an instrument used to measure **relative humidity.** It consists of a **dry-bulb thermometer** and a **wet-bulb thermometer.** Also called hygrometer.

R

Radar. *See* **Conventional radar.**

Radiation fog: fog that forms when a warm, moist layer of air exists at the surface and drier air lies above.

Radiational cooling: the loss of heat by the ground, to the atmosphere.

Radioactive dating: a technique used to determine the age of rocks that contain radioactive elements, which works on the principle that radioactive nuclei emit high-energy particles over time.

Radiosonde: an instrument package carried aloft on a small helium- or hydrogen-filled balloon. It measures temperature, **air pressure,** and **relative humidity** from the ground to a maximum height of 19 miles (30 kilometers).

Rain band: a tightly coiled band of **thunderstorm cloud**s that spirals around the **eye** of a **hurricane.**

Rain gauge: a container that catches rain and measures the amount of rainfall.

Rain-shadow effect: the uneven distribution of precipitation across a mountain, with most of the precipitation falling on the **windward slope** and very little falling on the **leeward slope**.

Rainbow: an arc of light, separated into its constituent colors, that stretches across the sky.

Rainforest climate: a **climate** type that is warm and rainy all year long.

Rawinsonde: a **radiosonde** that emits a signal so that its location can be tracked by radar on the ground. It measures changes in wind speed and wind direction with altitude.

Reduction to sea level: a process that standardizes **air pressure** readings with regard to altitude, making it possible to isolate differences in air pressure over horizontal distances.

Reflection: the process by which light both strikes a surface, and bounces off that surface, at the same angle.

Refraction: the bending of light as it is transmitted between two transparent media of different densities.

Regional winds. *See* **Mesoscale winds**

Relative humidity: A measure of humidity as a percentage of the total moisture a given volume of air, at a particular temperature, can hold.

Resolution: a measure of the precision of a weather forecast. The higher the resolution, the smaller the area for which the forecast is relevant.

Return stroke: lightning that surges up from the ground to meet the **stepped leader,** when the stepped leader is about 325 feet (40 meters) above the ground.

Ribbon lightning: lightning that appears to sway from the cloud. It is produced when the wind blows the **ionized channel** so that its position shifts between **return stroke**s.

Ridge: a northward crest in the wave-like flow of **upper-air westerlies,** within which exists a high-pressure area.

Rime: an icy coating that contains trapped air and therefore appears whitish, on a solid surface.

Riming: the process by which water droplets freeze to a snowflake, trapping air pockets.

River flood: the overflowing of the banks of a river or stream. It may be caused by excessive rain, the springtime melting of snow, blockage of water flow due to ice, or the failure of a dam or aqueduct.

Roll cloud: a cloud that looks like a giant, elongated cylinder lying on its side, that is rolling forward. It follows in the wake of a **gust front.**

Rossby waves: Long waves that are components of **upper-air westerlies.** At any given time, the entire hemisphere is encircled by just two to five Rossby waves.

S

Saffir-Simpson Hurricane Intensity Scale: the scale that ranks **hurricane**s according to their intensity, using the following criteria: **air pressure** at the **eye** of the storm; range of wind speeds; potential height of the **storm surge;** and the potential damage caused.

Saltation: the wind-driven migration of particles along the ground and through the air.

Sand dune: a mound of sand that is comprised of billions of sand grains, produced by a strong wind blowing in a fairly constant direction over time.

Sand ripples: wavy designs, running perpendicular to the direction of the wind, formed by the motion of sand along the surface of a **sand dune.**

Santa Ana winds: warm, dry, easterly or northeasterly winds that blow through southern California at a speed of at least 29 mph (46 kph).

Sastrugi: snow ripples (similar to **sand ripples**), up to 20 inches (50 centimeters) high, that form in Antarctica and other very cold places.

Saturated: air that has 100 percent **relative humidity.**

Saturation point: the point at which a given volume of air contains the maximum possible amount of water vapor. The addition of more water vapor at that point will result in **condensation.**

Savanna climate: a **climate** type that is warm year-round with rainy summers and drought-prone dry winters, and receives less yearly rainfall than a **monsoon climate.**

Scattering: multi-directional **reflection** of light by minute particles in the air.

Sea breeze: the gentle wind that blows from over the sea to the shore during the day, due to differences in **air pressure** above each surface.

Sea fog: a type of **advection fog** that only occurs at sea and in coastal areas. It is produced by the interaction of two adjacent **ocean currents** that have different temperatures.

Season: a period of year characterized by certain weather conditions, such as temperature and **precipitation,** as well as the number of hours of sunlight each day.

Secondary air pollutant: an **air pollutant** produced when a **primary air pollutant** undergoes chemical reactions with water, sunlight, or other pollutants.

Sector plate: a starry-shaped **snowflake.**

Seif dune: a very steep **barchan dune** with a very pronounced crescent shape, that either exists singly or in a connected line.

Semipermanent highs and lows: the four large pressure areas (two high-pressure and two low-pressure), situated throughout the **Northern Hemisphere,** that undergo slight shifts in position, and major changes in strength, throughout the year.

Severe blizzard: a **blizzard** in which wind speeds exceed 45 mph (72 kph), snowfall is heavy, and the temperature is no higher than 10°F (-12°C).

Severe thunderstorm: a **thunderstorm** that produces some combination of high winds, **hail, flash flood**s, and **tornado**es.

Sheet lightning: lightning that illuminates a cloud or a portion of a cloud.

Shelf cloud: a fan-shaped cloud with a flat base that forms along the edge of a **gust front.**

Short waves: The approximately twelve ripples that exist within each **Rossby wave.**

Shower: a spell of heavy, localized rainfall, that only occurs in warm weather.

Shrinking stage: the stage of **tornado** development during which the tornado's funnel narrows and tilts, and the tornado's path of destruction decreases in width.

Sinkhole: a dramatic example of **subsidence,** such as when roof of a cave collapses, that forms a large depression.

Sirocco: a hot dry, dusty southeasterly wind out of North Africa that travels across the Mediterranean Sea. It reaches Sicily and southern Italy as warm and humid wind.

Ski report: a specialized weather report that provides forecasts for popular ski destinations.

Sling psychrometer: an instrument that measures **relative humidity.** It consists of a **dry-bulb thermometer** and a **wet-bulb thermometer** mounted side by side on a metal strip, which rotates on a handle at one end.

Smog: a word created by combining "smoke" and "fog," that describes a thick layer of air pollution.

Snow dune: a large drift of snow, similar to a **sand dune.**

Snow fence: a device placed in fields and along highways that slows the wind and reduces the blowing and drifting of snow.

Snow grains: small, soft, white grains of ice that form within **stratus** clouds and only fall to the ground in small amounts. The frozen equivalent of **drizzle.**

Snow pellets: white pieces of icy matter that measure between .08 and .19 inches (.2 and .5 centimeters) in diameter. Snow pellets fall in showers and feel brittle and crunchy underfoot. Also called graupel or soft hail.

Snow ripples: long wavelike patterns in the snow that run perpendicular to the direction of the wind.

Snow squall: a brief but heavy snow shower, similar in intensity to a rain **shower,** accompanied by strong surface winds.

Snowflake: a hexagonal assemblage of ice crystals that is the basic unit of snow.

Snowroller: a lumpy, spherical or cylindrical mass of snow, generally less than 1 foot in diameter, formed by the wind.

Soft hail. *See* **Snow pellets**

Sounding: an analysis of temperature and humidity readings at various heights throughout the **troposphere.**

Southern Hemisphere: the half of Earth that lies south of the equator.

Southern Oscillation: a shifting pattern of **air pressure** between the eastern and western edges of the Pacific Ocean in the Southern Hemisphere.

Specific heat: the amount of heat required to raise one gram of a substance by 1°C (1.8°F).

Spontaneous nucleation: the process by which water freezes into ice crystals in the absence of **freezing nuclei,** which occurs at temperatures below -40°F (-40°C). Also called homogeneous nucleation.

Squall line: a band of thunderstorms that runs parallel to a **cold front,** either coinciding with the cold front or existing up to 200 miles (322 kilometers) in front of it.

Stable air layer: an atmospheric layer through which an **air parcel** cannot rise or descend.

Station circle. *See* **Weather station entry**

Stationary front: the dividing line between two stationary **air mass**es. It occurs when cold air comes in contact with warm air, yet neither side budges.

Steam devils: steam fog that forms in dense, rising, swirling columns over large bodies of water during the winter.

Steam fog: a type of **evaporation fog** that forms over a body of water.

Steppe climate: a semi-dry **climate** type that receives less than 20 inches (50 centimeters) of rainfall annually and exists in the **rain shadow** of a mountain range or at the edge of a desert.

Stepped leader: an invisible stream of electrons that initiates a **lightning** stroke. A stepped leader surges from the negatively charged region of a cloud, down through the base of the cloud, and travels in a stepwise fashion toward the ground.

Storm chaser: a professional or amateur weather-watcher who follows the path of a **tornado,** attempting to sight it and study its effects.

Storm surge: a wall of water, with huge waves, that sweeps on shore when the **eye** of the **hurricane** passes overhead.

Storm tide: the combined height of water that sweeps on shore in a **hurricane** due to the **storm surge** and the tide.

Stratiform: a cloud formation that appears as a continuous flat sheet or layer.

Stratocumulus: puffy clouds that exist in layers, at low levels of the **troposphere.**

Stratosphere: the second-lowest layer of Earth's atmosphere, from about 9 to 40 miles (15 to 65 kilometers) above ground.

Stratus: gloomy, gray, featureless sheets of clouds that cover the entire sky, at low levels of the **troposphere.**

Sublimation: the process by which water changes directly from a solid to a gas, without first going through the liquid phase.

Subpolar climate: a cold, northern type of **climate** that has long, harsh winters and short, cool summers.

Subsidence: the lowering of land in coastal areas, which makes them susceptible to flooding.

Suction vortices: small vortices within a single **tornado** that continually form and dissipate as the tornado moves along, creating the tornado's strongest surface winds.

Sundogs: one or two patches of light that appear on either or both sides of the sun. Sundogs are produced by the refraction of sunlight that shines through platelike ice crystals. Also called mock suns or parahelia.

Sunspot: a dark area of magnetic disturbance on the sun's surface.

Supercell storm: the most destructive and long-lasting form of **severe thunderstorm,** arising from a single, powerful **convective cell.** It is characterized by strong **tornado**es, heavy rain, and **hail** the size of golfballs or larger.

Supercooled water: water that remains in the liquid state below the freezing point.

Superior mirage: a cold-weather **mirage** that appears as a taller and closer, and sometimes inverted, image of a distant object.

T

Temperate climate: a **climate** type that has four distinct seasons with warm, humid summers and cold, snowy winters.

Terminal velocity: the constant speed at which an object falls when the upward force of air resistance equals the downward pull of gravity. An object can never fall at a rate faster than its terminal velocity. Also called maximum rate of fall.

Thermal: a pocket of rising, warm air that is produced by uneven heating of the ground.

Thermograph: an instrument consisting of a **thermometer** and a needle that etches on a rotating drum, continually recording the temperature.

Thermometer: an instrument used to measure temperature. It consists of a vacuum-sealed narrow glass tube with a bulb in the bottom containing mercury or red-dyed alcohol. Also called dry-bulb thermometer.

Thermosphere: the layer of Earth's atmosphere, between 50 and 200 miles (80 and 320 kilometers) above ground, in which temperatures reach 1,800°F (330°C).

Thunder: the sound wave that results when the intense heating due to **lightning** causes the air to expand explosively.

Thunderstorm: a relatively small but intense storm system, that produces moderate-to-strong winds, heavy rain, and **lightning,** and sometimes **hail** and **tornado**es.

Thunderstorm cloud. *See* **Cumulonimbus**

Topography: the shape and height of Earth's surface features.

Tornadic waterspout: a **tornado** that forms over land and travels over water. Tornadic waterspouts are relatively rare and are the most intense form of **waterspout**s.

Tornado: a rapidly spinning column of air that extends from a **thunderstorm cloud** to the ground. Also called a twister.

Tornado cyclone: a spinning column of air that protrudes through the base of a **thunderstorm cloud.**

Tornado family: a group of **tornado**es that develops from a single **thunderstorm.**

Tornado outbreak: the emergence of a **tornado family.** Tornado outbreaks are responsible for the greatest amount of tornado-related damage.

Trade winds: the winds that blow throughout the tropics, circulating air between the equator and 30 degrees latitude, North and South.

Transpiration: the process by which plants emit water through tiny pores in the underside of their leaves.

Transverse dunes: a series of connected **barchan dunes,** which appear as tall, elongated crescents of sand running perpendicular to the **prevailing wind.**

Traveler's report: a specialized weather report that tells what the weather is like at popular vacation spots and major cities around the world.

Tropical cyclone: a storm system that forms in the tropics, in the absence of **fronts.**

Tropical depression: the weakest form of **tropical cyclone,** characterized by rotating bands of clouds and **thunderstorm**s with maximum sustained winds of 38 mph (61 kph) or less.

Tropical disturbance: a cluster of **thunderstorm**s that is beginning to rotate.

Tropical squall cluster: a **squall line** that forms over tropical waters.

Tropical storm: a **tropical cyclone** weaker than a **hurricane,** with organized bands of rotating **thunderstorm**s and maximum sustained winds of 39 to 73 mph (63 to 117 kph).

Tropopause: the boundary between the **troposphere** and the **stratosphere,** between 30,000 and 40,000 feet (9 and 12 kilometers) above ground.

Troposphere: the lowest atmospheric layer, where clouds exist and virtually all weather occurs.

Trough: a southward dip in the wave-like flow of **upper-air westerlies,** within which exists a low-pressure area.

Tsunami: the largest type of water wave, generated by a submarine earthquake, landslide, or volcanic eruption.

Tundra climate: a **climate** type that has bitterly cold winters and cool summers. For at least one month of the year the average temperature is above freezing.

Typhoon: the name for a **hurricane** that occurs in the western North Pacific or China Sea region.

U

Unsaturated: air that has less than 100 percent **relative humidity.**

Unstable air layer: an atmospheric layer through which an **air parcel** can rise or descend.

Updraft: a column of air blowing upward, inside a **vertical cloud.**

Upper-air westerlies: global-scale, upper-air winds that flow in waves heading west-to-east (but also shifting north and south) through the **middle latitudes** of the **Northern Hemisphere.**

Upslope fog: fog formed by the slow passage of a moist **air parcel** up the side of a hill or mountain.

Upwelling: the rising up of cold waters from the depths of the ocean.

V

Valley breeze: an uphill wind that forms during the day as the valley air is heated and rises. Also called anabatic wind.

Valley fog: fog that forms when cold air sinks into a valley and, due to the presence of a river or stream, picks up moisture.

Vapor pressure: the pressure exerted by a vapor when it is in equilibrium with its liquid or solid. The vapor pressure determines the rate at which molecules of a substance will change phases.

Veering wind: a wind that shifts direction, clockwise, with height.

Ventifact: a rock, boulder, or canyon wall that has been sculpted by wind and wind-blown sand.

Vertical cloud: a cloud that develops upward to great heights. Vertical clouds are the products of sudden, forceful uplifts of small pockets of warm air.

Virga: Rain that falls from clouds but evaporates in mid-air under conditions of very low humidity.

Vortex: a vertical axis of extremely low pressure around which winds rotate.

W

Wall cloud: a roughly circular, rotating cloud that protrudes from the base of a **thunderstorm cloud** and is often a precursor to a **tornado.**

Warm clouds: clouds that exist in the tropics that are too warm to contain ice.

Warm front: the line behind which a warm **air mass** is advancing, and in front of which a cold air mass is retreating.

Warm occlusion: a rare type of **occluded front,** in which a relatively warm **air mass** overtakes a colder air mass.

Warning: a severe weather advisory that means that a storm has been sighted and may strike a specific area.

Watch: a severe weather advisory that means that while a storm does not yet exist, conditions are ripe for one to develop.

Water cycle: the continuous exchange of water between the atmosphere and the oceans and landmasses on the surface. Also called hydrologic cycle.

Waterspout: a rapidly rotating column of air that forms over a large body of water, extending from the base of a cloud to the surface of the water.

Weather aircraft: aircraft that carry weather instruments and collect data in the upper levels of the **troposphere.** They are primarily used to probe storm clouds, within which they measure temperature, **air pressure,** and wind speed and direction.

Weather forecast: a prediction of what the weather will be like in the future, based on present and past conditions.

Weather map: a map of a nation or group of nations, on which **weather station entries** are plotted. By looking at a weather map, a **meteorologist** can determine the locations of **fronts,** regions of high- and low-pressure, the dividing line between temperatures below freezing and above freezing, and the movement of storm systems. Also called surface analysis.

Weather modification: the use of artificial means to alter atmospheric phenomena.

Weather satellite: a satellite equipped with infrared and visible imaging equipment, that provides views of storms and continuously monitors weather conditions around the planet.

Weather station entry: the information collected at an individual weather station, recorded in **international weather symbols,** and placed on a **weather map.** Also called station circle.

Westerlies: Global-scale surface winds that travel from the southwest to the northeast in the **Northern Hemisphere,** and from the northwest to the southeast in the **Southern Hemisphere,** between about 30 and 60 degrees latitude.

Wet-bulb depression: the difference in temperatures measured by a **dry-bulb thermometer** and a **wet-bulb thermometer** at a given time.

Wet-bulb thermometer: a **thermometer** with wet muslin wrapped around the bulb, used to measure the temperature of **saturated** air.

Whirlwinds. *See* **Dust devils**

Whiteout: a condition in which falling, drifting, and blowing snow reduce visibility to almost zero.

Wind profiler: a specialized **Doppler radar,** resembling a giant metal checkerboard, that measures the speed and direction of **winds aloft.**

Wind shear: a condition in which a vertical layer of air is sandwiched between two other vertical layers, each of which is traveling at a different speed and/or direction, causing the sandwiched air layer to roll.

Wind sock: a cone-shaped cloth bag open on both ends, through which wind flows, that is used to determine the direction of the wind.

Wind turbine: a relatively small **windmill** with thin, propeller-like blades.

Wind vane: a free-swinging horizontal metal bar with a vertically oriented, flat metal sheet at one end and an arrow on the other end, that is used to determine the direction of the wind.

Wind waves: water waves that are driven by the wind.

Windchill equivalent temperature (WET): the temperature at which the body would lose an equivalent amount of heat, if there were no wind. Also called windchill index.

Windchill factor: the cooling effect on the body due to a combination of wind and temperature.

Winds aloft: winds that blow in the middle and upper levels of the **troposphere.**

Windward slope: the westward side of a mountain, on which warm air ascends, forms clouds, and yields precipitation.

PICTURE CREDITS

The photographs and illustrations appearing in *The Complete Weather Resource* were received from the following sources:

On the front cover of Volume 1: Virga (**FMA Research, Inc. Reproduced by permission.**); on the front cover of Volume 2: Aurora borealis (**JLM Visuals. Reproduced by permission.**); on the front cover of Volume 3: Power plant smokestack (**FMA Research, Inc. Reproduced by permission.**); on the back covers: weather map (**JLM Visuals. Reproduced by permission.**).

Courtesy of Gale Research: pp. 2, 12, 413, 501; **Corbis-Bettmann. Reproduced by permission:** pp. 8, 11, 16, 17, 205, 206, 379, 392, 475, 497, 519; **FMA Research, Inc. Reproduced by permission:** pp. 10, 50, 58, 59, 69, 78, 79, 80, 81, 82, 84, 85, 86, 87, 88, 89, 90, 93, 96, 97, 98, 99, 100, 102, 103, 105, 110, 111, 112, 113, 115, 116, 118, 119, 128, 130, 140, 147, 183, 185, 186, 193, 199, 201, 224, 233, 236, 255, 320, 332, 334, 335, 336, 337, 373, 383, 384, 396, 399, 402, 409, 411, 414, 416, 419, 432, 464, 476, 510, 520; **Mary Evans Picture Library. Reproduced by permission:** pp. 14, 15, 65; **Culver Pictures, Inc. Reproduced by permission:** pp. 20, 480; **Courtesy of Weather Service International Corporation. Reproduced by permission:** pp. 44, 282, 417, 418, 431; **JLM Visuals. Reproduced by permission:** pp. 52, 133, 305, 325, 380, 456, 459, 466, 468, 473, 484, 502, 507, 513; **Photograph by Cecil Keen. Reproduced by permission:** p. 101; **Photograph by Joanne Pease. Reproduced by permission:** p. 134; **Reuters/Corbis-Bettmann. Reproduced by permission:** pp. 142, 275, 311, 518; **Photograph by Mark Uliasz. Reproduced by permission:** p. 143; **Courtesy of Phillis Engelbert:** pp. 188, 462; **W. A. Bentley:** p.

195; **UPI/Corbis-Bettmann. Reproduced by permission:** pp. 228, 294, 309, 312, 314, 492, 508, 517; **AP/Wide World Photos. Reproduced by permission:** p. 238; **National Severe Storms Laboratory. Reproduced by permission:** p. 244; **Photograph by Herbert Stein. Reproduced by permission:** p. 256; **National Aeronautics and Space Administration (NASA). Reproduced by permission:** p. 263; **Paramount/The Kobal Collection. Reproduced by permission:** p. 279; **Photograph by SIU. National Audubon Society Collection/Photo Researchers, Inc. Reproduced by permission:** p. 306; **Massachusetts Institute of Technology (MIT). Reproduced by permission:** pp. 374, 377; **National Weather Service. Reproduced by permission:** p. 428; **U. S. Department of Transportation. Reproduced by permission:** p. 429; **Courtesy of WNBC News Channel 4. Reproduced by permission:** p. 435; **Twentieth Century Fox/The Kobal Collection. Reproduced by permission:** p. 458.

All other diagrams were created by Accurate Art, Inc., Holbrook, New York.

WHAT IS WEATHER?

Weather plays an important role in all our lives. It dictates how we dress, what outdoor activities we can undertake, and even what our moods are. Clearly, weather is on everyone's mind, for it is one of the most-talked about topics everywhere. We all know what weather brings: wind, rain, snow, thunderstorms, clear skies. But what causes the weather? Where does it all come from?

Throughout this section, we will examine the various factors that interact to bring about weather conditions. As a general introduction, suffice it to say that all forms of weather are produced by complex, constantly changing conditions in Earth's atmosphere. Yet the driving force behind the weather is located far, far away. That force is the sun.

IT STARTS WITH THE SUN

The sun continually generates energy, which escapes from its surface and flows through space. After traveling 93 million miles (149 million kilometers) solar energy reaches Earth. It warms all of Earth's atmosphere, but some parts more than others. The area of Earth that receives the sun's rays most directly, the equatorial region, is heated the most. The poles, conversely, never receive sunlight directly. Sunlight strikes the poles only at a steep angle. Hence they are warmed the least.

Another factor that determines how much solar energy strikes any particular part of Earth at any time is the **season.** Most places in the world have four seasons: winter, summer, spring, and fall. In winter, the sun shines for the fewest hours per day and never gets very high in the sky. In summer, day is longer than night and the sun shines high in the sky. In spring and fall the sun rises to an intermediate height, and there are roughly the same number of hours of daylight as darkness.

The change in seasons is caused by a combination of Earth's tilt and its yearly journey around the sun. Earth's axis of rotation is tilted 23.4 degrees away from the perpendicular. As you can see in Figure 1, at different points along Earth's orbit around the sun, Earth's **Northern Hemisphere** (which includes the United States) is tilted either toward or away from the sun. For instance, on about June 21, the first day of summer, the Northern Hemisphere receives more sunlight than on any other day. On about December 21, the first day of winter, the **Southern Hemisphere** receives its greatest amount of sunlight.

There are two days each year when the hemispheres receive equal amounts of sunlight. They are around March 21, the vernal **equinox,** and around September 23, the autumnal equinox. These two days mark the start of spring and fall.

The uneven heating of the atmosphere is the factor that sets the atmosphere in motion. Air moves through the atmosphere in such a way as to even out the distribution of heat around the planet, with warm air moving from the equator to cold areas at the poles and cold air back toward

Figure 1: The seasons.

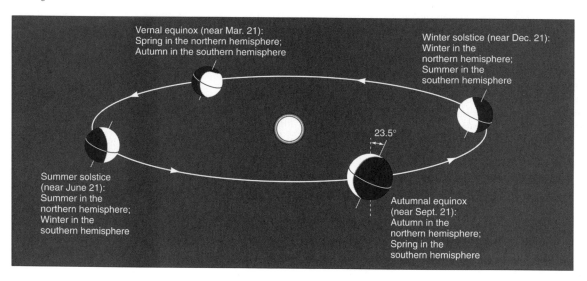

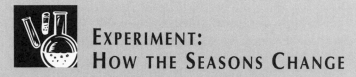

EXPERIMENT:
HOW THE SEASONS CHANGE

Place a lamp (minus the lampshade) on the desk in front of you. Now take a tennis ball or a ping pong ball and draw a horizontal line around its middle. This line represents Earth's equator. Mark an "N" on the top half of the ball (for the Northern Hemisphere) and an "S" on the bottom half (for the Southern Hemisphere).

First hold the ball with the "N" pointing straight up and the "S" pointing down. Now tilt the ball so the "N" is tilted slightly away from the perpendicular. This arrangement represents the 23.4 degree tilt of Earth's axis away from the perpendicular. Hold the ball this way in front of the light and move it in a circle around the light in this order: to the right of the light, behind the light, to the left, and finally to the front again.

You'll notice that when the ball is to the right of the light (similar to Earth on the first day of winter), light from the lamp strikes the "S" half of the ball more directly than it does the "N" half. When the ball is directly behind or in front of the light (representing the start of spring and fall, respectively), light strikes both "N" and "S" halves at the same angle. And when the ball is to the left of the light, light strikes the "N" half more directly. This position marks the start of summer in the Northern Hemisphere.

the equator. The movement of air between the equator and the poles is influenced by other factors as well, such as differences in composition of air over land and sea and Earth's rotation. The result is a complex web of air currents whirling around the globe—the ingredients of weather.

WHEN SOLAR ENERGY STRIKES EARTH

Energy that comes from the sun is often referred to as "sunlight." Yet, it is really a combination of many types of **electromagnetic radiation.** Electromagnetic radiation is energy in the form of waves of electricity and magnetism. Solar energy that reaches Earth's surface is made up almost entirely of visible light (light we can see), and infrared radiation. Infrared radiation is a form of electromagnetic radiation with a wavelength longer than that of visible light and that takes the form of heat. Small amounts of X-rays, ultraviolet rays, and radio waves from the sun also penetrate into Earth's atmosphere.

Only two forms of solar energy reach and heat up the lower levels of atmosphere and Earth's surface. These are visible light and infrared radiation. They are the only two forms of solar energy that affect Earth's weather. When radiation is absorbed by gas molecules in the atmosphere, by clouds or by the ground, it is converted to heat.

Most X-rays and ultraviolet rays are absorbed high in Earth's atmosphere and never reach the surface. This is fortunate for humans, since a large dose of either type of radiation would be deadly. Radio waves also penetrate the atmosphere, but in such tiny amounts that they have no warming effect on Earth.

Only about two-thirds of the total solar energy reaching Earth's outer atmosphere is absorbed by Earth. One half of that radiation is absorbed by the atmosphere and the other half by Earth's surface. Ultraviolet radiation is selectively absorbed by the **ozone layer,** an atmospheric layer that exists between 25 and 40 miles (40 and 64 kilometers) above Earth's surface. Infrared radiation is absorbed by clouds and gases in the lowest atmospheric levels and then re-radiated in all directions.

Most of the solar radiation that reaches Earth's surface is in the form of visible light. About two-thirds of that light is absorbed by living and non-living materials and transformed into heat. This heat causes snow and ice to melt and water to evaporate.

About one-third of solar radiation striking Earth is reflected back into space. A number of factors are responsible for this effect. One of the most important is clouds. When solar energy strikes a thick cloud, as much as 95 percent of the energy is reflected. Thinner clouds turn away up to 50 percent of the radiation that strikes them.

On the ground, the greatest reflectors of sunlight are snow and ice. Snow and ice reflect up to 95 percent of the solar energy that strikes them. Thus, air is colder when there's snow on the ground. Water, on the other hand, is a good absorber of energy. Water reflects only 10 percent of the solar energy that strikes it. Sand reflects more radiation than water (about 15 to 40 percent), but much less than snow.

THE EARTH ALSO RADIATES HEAT

Solar energy that reaches Earth's surface in the form of visible light is re-radiated in the form of infrared radiation (heat). Heat leaves Earth's surface and is absorbed by clouds and water vapor in the air. Clouds absorb large amounts of infrared radiation, which is the reason why cloudy nights tend to be warmer than clear nights, all other things being equal. Clouds radiate infrared energy in all directions, throughout the atmosphere, back toward Earth, and out into space.

All parts of Earth's surface are constantly absorbing and emitting heat. For the temperature to remain constant at any one location, the surface must absorb and emit energy at the same rate. When absorption outpaces emission, the surface warms. You can experience this effect when you walk on an asphalt parking lot in your bare feet. When emission outpaces absorption, the surface cools. This effect occurs at night when there is no incoming sunlight to offset the heat radiating from the ground.

Earth maintains a long-term balancing act with regard to heat. Over a period of years, the quantity of heat absorbed is almost identical to the quantity released back into space. Some scientists, however, believe that a slight warming trend has begun in recent decades. This effect may be caused by increased amounts of certain gases in the air, primarily carbon dioxide. Carbon dioxide and other gases formed during industrial processes on Earth trap heat (for more information on greenhouse effect, see "Human Activity and the Future," page 502).

THE MECHANICS OF HEAT TRANSFER

The primary way that heat is transferred in the atmosphere is by **convection.** Convection is the movement of masses of air caused by differences in temperature. It can be explained by two key concepts. First, heat causes air molecules to move more quickly. Second, warm air rises.

When air is heated, the molecules within it move rapidly and spread out. As a result, warm air loses density and becomes thinner and lighter. The surrounding cool air, which is denser, slides beneath the warm air, pushing it upwards. As the warm air rises, it cools. When it is no longer warmer than the air around it, it stops rising.

You can perform a simple experiment demonstrating the expansion and contraction of air with changing temperature. Blow up a balloon and put it in the refrigerator. After a while, take it out and you will observe that it has shrunk. Now place this balloon in a warm spot, where you can see that it will slowly expand. This experiment shows that when a fluid is heated, be it a liquid or a gas, its molecules move apart and become less dense. If the molecules move fast enough, they can push the material that surrounds them (in this case, the balloon). When the fluid cools, its molecules move more slowly, come closer together again, and the fluid takes up less volume, even though the number of molecules never changed.

Convection is a critical element in the formation of weather patterns. It is the process that carries warm air up from the ground, to be replaced by cold air. The cold air is then warmed and cycles upward again.

Heat can also be transferred by a second method called **conduction.** This method depends upon collisions between individual molecules, in which heat is transferred from a fast-moving, warm molecule to a slow-moving, cold molecule. As the cold molecule is heated, it also moves more quickly, and a chain reaction of molecular heat transfer ensues.

Conduction is a very slow process because, even in the densest layer of the atmosphere, collisions between molecules are relatively rare.

HEAT AND TEMPERATURE

Most people consider heat and temperature to be the same. After all, when you raise the temperature in your oven, you can feel the heat at the oven door. However, as we will see, while heat and temperature are closely related, there are differences between them.

WHAT'S THE DIFFERENCE?

In order to answer that question, we must first explain the concept of **kinetic energy**—the energy of motion. All substances are made of tiny particles (molecules or atoms) that are in constant motion. Motion ceases only at **absolute zero,** -459°F (-273°C). Heat is defined as the *total* kinetic energy of a substance, whereas temperature is the *average* kinetic energy of a substance. (For information on temperature scales and measurement, see "Forecasting," page 389.)

The crux of this distinction is that heat takes into account the total volume of a substance. That is, given two volumes of the same liquid at the same temperature, the larger one contains more heat because it contains more matter. The larger volume contains a greater number of moving molecules and, hence, more total kinetic energy.

This concept is best explained by way of example. Take two vessels of liquid: a cup of coffee that's 140°F (60°C) and a bathtub of water that's 85°F (30°C). If you let them both cool to room temperature, you'll see that the coffee cools much more quickly than does the water. The reason for this difference is that the water in the bathtub possesses a large quantity (relative to the coffee cup) of kinetic energy, which it must lose in order to cool down. The coffee cup, which contains relatively little kinetic energy, cools quickly. Although the coffee had a higher starting temperature (*average* kinetic energy) than the bath water, the bath water possessed more heat (*total* kinetic energy).

SPECIFIC HEAT

The **specific heat** of a substance is the amount of heat required to raise the temperature of 0.0353 ounce (1 gram) of the substance by 1.8°F (1°C). The amount of heat (measured in units called calories) necessary to raise the temperature differs from substance to substance.

The specific heat of a substance is measured relative to that of water: It takes 1 calorie to raise 1 gram of liquid water 1°C. Water, therefore, has a specific heat of 1.0. This is one of the largest specific heats of any naturally occurring substance.

By way of comparison, the specific heat of ice at 32°F (0°C) is .478; wood is .420; sand is .188; dry air is .171; and silver is .056. Thus, it can be seen that it takes much less heat to raise the temperature of sand than it does to raise the temperature of water. To illustrate this point, if you're at the beach on a sunny day, you'll notice that the sand heats up much more quickly, and feels much hotter, than the water.

LATENT HEAT

In the discussion on specific heat, we explained that a large amount of heat is needed to raise the temperature of water even slightly. This effect is magnified when water undergoes a phase change. A phase change occurs when a substance changes between any two of the three phases: liquid, solid, or gas. During a phase change, water or ice absorbs or emits very large amounts of heat energy without any corresponding change in temperature. The energy associated with a phase change of water is called **latent heat.**

The reason this heat is called "latent" is that it does not perform a warming function, but instead is "stored" or "hidden" as it produces a phase change. A tremendous amount of energy is absorbed in the process of melting ice or of evaporating or boiling water. Conversely, when water freezes or when water vapor condenses, that heat energy is released back into the environment. To demonstrate this concept, place a cup of water and a cup of ice—both at 32°F (0°C)—side by side. You will find that it takes much

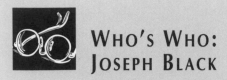

WHO'S WHO:
JOSEPH BLACK

As a graduate student, Scottish chemist Joseph Black (1728–1799) discovered the existence of carbon dioxide, which he called "fixed air." He demonstrated that carbon dioxide could not sustain the flame of a burning candle. In 1760, Black also was the first person to explain the concept of specific heat (see page 7), that each substance requires a specific amount of heat, particular to that substance, to raise its temperature 1°C.

Black, however, is most famous for solving the mystery of latent heat. He was first drawn to the question by the finding by German physicist Gabriel Daniel Fahrenheit that water can remain in the liquid state even below its freezing point. This state is called **supercooled water.** On striking a surface, supercooled raindrops freeze. The freezing of water is a process that occurs when heat is lost. While heat loss can usually be measured with a thermometer, in this case the water froze with no accompanying drop in temperature. This discovery led Black to the conclusion that water possesses hidden or "latent" energy that comes and goes as water changes phases.

In one experiment Black placed a tub of ice and a tub of water, both at 32°F (0°C), side by side. He found that the water warmed to room temperature much more quickly than the ice. Black conducted similar experiments with vaporization, showing that it took far less heat to increase the temperature of liquid water than to change it into a gas.

"The effect of heat... consists, not in warming the surrounding bodies, but in rendering the ice fluid," wrote Black. "So, in the case of boiling, the heat absorbed does not warm surrounding bodies, but converts the water into vapor."

For further reading on latent heat and Joseph Black, see Williams, Richard. "The Mystery of Disappearing Heat." Weatherwise. Aug./Sept. 1996: 28–29.

longer for the ice to reach room temperature than it does the water. The reason is that ice must first absorb enough heat to transform it to water.

Latent heat is also responsible for keeping a cold drink *with* ice colder than a cold drink *without* ice. It works like this: as heat is added to the beverage, it breaks down the crystal structure of the molecules of ice. It changes ice from a solid to a liquid without changing the temperature of the surrounding liquid. If heat were added to a drink without ice, that heat would warm the liquid instead.

Latent heat has important implications on a global scale. More than half of the solar energy that strikes Earth is stored in the form of latent heat. Since ice is able to store large amounts of solar energy in the form of latent heat, it is slow to melt. Imagine if the Arctic or Antarctic ice caps were to melt just because of the heat they absorbed on one mild day. We would be faced with unfathomable floods! Similarly, latent heat of vaporization is what accounts for the fact that the oceans do not evaporate.

WINDCHILL

On blustery winter days, weather forecasts usually include the **windchill factor,** as well as the temperature. Wind magnifies the effects of low temperature, the reason being that moving air removes heat from the body more quickly than does still air. The body is ordinarily surrounded by a very thin layer of still air, called the boundary layer. While you constantly lose some heat through the boundary layer by **conduction,** this process is very slow. With increased wind, however, the boundary layer is reduced in thickness and heat loss accelerates.

The danger of **frostbite** in cold, windy conditions has prompted weather forecasters to include an index called the **windchill equivalent temperature** (WET), also called the "windchill index" (see Figure 2). This value represents the temperature at which the body would lose an equivalent amount of heat if there were no wind. For instance, if it were 32°F (0°C) with winds blowing at 15 miles per hour (mph), or 24 kilometers per hour (kph), the WET would be 15°F (-9°C). If it were 0°F (-18°C) and the wind was blowing at 10 mph (16 kph), the WET would be -20°F (-30°C).

THE ATMOSPHERE: WHERE WEATHER OCCURS

The atmosphere is an enormous ocean of air that extends more than 600 miles (1,000 kilometers) above Earth's surface. Yet relative to the diameter of Earth, it is no thicker than a coat of paint. The atmosphere is not only where all weather occurs, but it is what sustains life on Earth.

The atmosphere contains the air we breathe and the water vapor that drives weather patterns. It shields us from most of the lethal components of the sun's rays while allowing through the harmless components. It regulates the temperature of the planet, keeping us from getting burned up by the sun's heat during the day or frozen to death during the dark night. In addition, the atmosphere protects us from most of the potentially devastating meteors (space debris, also known as "shooting stars").

The atmosphere is made of 78 percent nitrogen, 21 percent oxygen, and 1 percent argon, with minute quantities of water vapor, carbon dioxide, and other gases. It is held to Earth by the force of gravity, which acts most strongly close to the surface. For this reason, the pressure and density of gases in the atmosphere decreases with altitude (height). In fact, half of the mass of our atmosphere is contained within 4 miles (6 kilometers) of the planet's surface. While 99 percent of the atmosphere is calm, the air in the lowest 6 miles (10 kilometers) is constantly on the move.

LAYERS OF THE ATMOSPHERE

Beginning with a series of hot-air balloon experiments in the late 1800s, scientists have determined that the atmosphere is made up of five distinct layers. The bottom layer, where clouds exist and virtually all

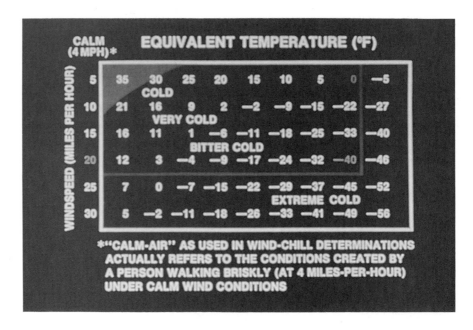

Figure 2: A windchill equivalent temperature chart.

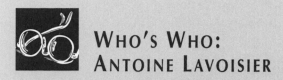

WHO'S WHO: ANTOINE LAVOISIER

French chemist Antoine-Laurent Lavoisier (1743–1794) is widely considered the father of modern chemistry. In the 1780s, Lavoisier identified the life-giving element present in air as "oxygen." Lavoisier is equally famous for describing what occurs when things burn, for formulating the system of naming chemical compounds, and for improving the accuracy of scientific methods.

Lavoisier was born into a wealthy family. He was originally trained to be a lawyer but quickly grew to dislike his vocation. Thus, he went on to study multiple areas of science—including chemistry, astronomy, mathematics, botany, and geology—with the leading French scientists of the time.

Through his experiments, Lavoisier learned that substances give off carbon dioxide when they burn. He also learned that oxygen has to be present in order for burning to occur. And Lavoisier isolated a second element present in large quantities in the air, which does not promote burning. To that element, originally discovered by the Scottish chemist Daniel Rutherford, he gave the name "azote." Today we know that element as nitrogen.

weather occurs, is called the **troposphere.** As you rise through the troposphere, the temperature drops rapidly. About 9 miles (15 kilometers) above ground you encounter the **stratosphere.** Jet planes cruise in the stratosphere to take advantage of strong winds found there and to reduce friction with air experienced in the troposphere. The temperature rises gradually from a low of about -75°F (-60°C) at the lowest level of the stratosphere to a high of about 32°F (0°C) at its upper boundary. The rate of temperature increase in the stratosphere rises sharply in the region between about 20 and 30 miles (30 and 50 kilometers). The reason for this change is the presence of a band of ozone in that portion of the stratosphere. Ozone is a

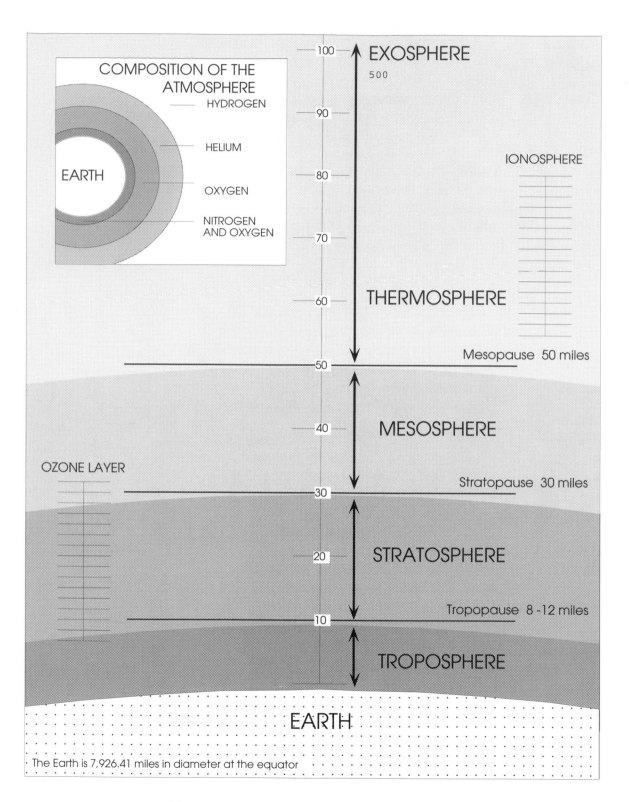

COMPOSITION OF THE ATMOSPHERE

EARTH

HYDROGEN

HELIUM

OXYGEN

NITROGEN AND OXYGEN

EXOSPHERE

500

100

90

80

70

60

IONOSPHERE

THERMOSPHERE

Mesopause 50 miles

50

MESOSPHERE

40

OZONE LAYER

Stratopause 30 miles

30

STRATOSPHERE

20

Tropopause 8-12 miles

10

TROPOSPHERE

EARTH

The Earth is 7,926.41 miles in diameter at the equator

form of oxygen that has three atoms per molecule instead of the usual two. It absorbs ultraviolet rays, which has a warming effect.

If you have heard of only one atmospheric layer, the **ozone layer** may be it. The reason is that the ozone layer is being destroyed by chemical pollutants. The loss of ozone from the stratosphere is a concern because it protects life on Earth from serious harm. For example, some forms of skin cancer are caused by exposure to certain kinds of ultraviolet radiation that are absorbed by ozone. Fortunately, governments around the world have now banned most of these dangerous substances, giving the protective shield an opportunity to regenerate. (For more information on ozone depletion, see "Human Activity and the Future," page 515)

The region of the atmosphere above the stratosphere is the **mesosphere.** This belt extends upwards from about 30 to 55 miles (50 to 90 kilometers) above Earth's surface. Within the mesosphere, the temperature falls from about 32°F (0°C) at its lower boundary to nearly -150°F (-100°C) at its upper boundary.

In the next higher zone, called the **thermosphere,** temperatures rise to about 1,800°F (1200°C). The thermosphere extends from a height of about 55 miles (90 kilometers) to about 300 miles (500 kilometers) above Earth's surface. The extreme heat in this layer burns up debris, such as meteors and non-operational satellites, falling toward Earth. Many of the molecules in both the upper mesosphere and lower thermosphere become **ionized** (electrically charged) by X-rays and ultraviolet rays in solar radiation. For this reason, that region is also called the **ionosphere.**

Continue upward and you'll reach the highest atmospheric layer, the **exosphere.** Molecules of gas in the exosphere break down into atoms. In addition, because gravitational attraction is so low, many molecules escape into space.

AIR PRESSURE AND WEATHER

Air pressure (also known as "barometric pressure" or "atmospheric pressure") is an all-important concept in the world of weather. Changes is air pressure are responsible for producing the winds, causing the development of clouds, and clearing the way for sunny skies. The air pressure at any given time provides weather forecasters with important clues about what the weather holds for the next several hours or days.

*Opposite page:
Figure 3: The gases that make up the several layers of Earth's atmosphere not only sustain life, they determine the type of life forms we see.*

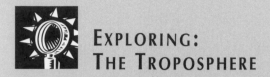

EXPLORING:
THE TROPOSPHERE

Much of what we know about temperature and wind conditions in the troposphere was collected by hot-air balloonists beginning in the late 1700s. Two of the most famous of these upper-air explorers were Englishmen James Glaisher and Robert Coxwell, who between 1862 and 1866 made twenty-eight flights over England.

The highest and riskiest ascent made by Glaisher and Coxwell was in September 1862. At an altitude of 29,500 feet (9,000 meters, or more than 5.5 miles), Glaisher lost consciousness from the lack of oxygen. The balloon continued to rise and at 37,500 feet (11,400 meters, or more than 7 miles) Coxwell was on the verge of passing out, too. At the last moment Coxwell managed to guide the balloon into a descent.

Unpiloted hot-air balloons were invented shortly thereafter. These balloons carried instruments to greater heights than humans could ever withstand. Using these balloons, French meteorologist Teisserenc de Bort learned that at about 9 miles (15 kilometers) above ground the air temperature no longer decreases, but begins to increase. De Bort had discovered the second atmospheric layer, the stratosphere.

WHAT IS AIR PRESSURE?

Simply put, air pressure is the pressure exerted by the weight of air over an area of Earth's surface. It is a function of the number of molecules of air in a given volume, the speed with which they are moving, and the frequency with which they collide. Although they are too small to see, air molecules are always in motion at tremendous speeds. In fact, at ground level, there are 400 sextillion (400 plus twenty-one zeroes) air molecules per cubic inch. And they are moving at an average speed of 1,090 mph (1,800 kph).

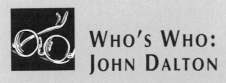

WHO'S WHO: JOHN DALTON

English chemist and Quaker John Dalton (1766–1844) chose to explore the simplest unit of matter: the atom. Dalton, in the early 1800s, postulated that all forms of matter, in all three phases (solid, liquid, and gas), are composed of tiny particles called atoms and that these atoms can combine to form "compound atoms." Italian chemist Amedeo Avogadro later changed the name of Dalton's compound atoms to "molecules," the name by which they are known today.

It was Dalton's interest in the weather that led to the development of his atomic theory. For fifty-seven years he kept daily records of temperature, **barometric pressure, dew point,** rainfall, and other conditions. He contemplated the nature of air and concluded that air, like every solid, liquid, or gas, is made up of tiny particles which he called "atoms."

Using his weather observations in combination with his atomic theory of air, Dalton learned how condensation occurs. First, he demonstrated that water vapor is a gas and can mix with other gases in the air. Then he proved that the amount of water that air can hold (the saturation point) depends upon the temperature of the air. From there he extrapolated that at every temperature, there is a corresponding saturation point. And by dividing the amount of water in the air by the amount of water at which air (at that temperature) would be saturated, he came up with an explanation of relative humidity.

The rapid movement of air molecules means that they frequently collide with one another and any objects they encounter. These collisions are responsible for air pressure. If air is heated, molecules move more quickly, collide more often, and cause an increase in pressure. If air is cooled, molecules move less rapidly, and air pressure decreases.

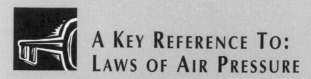

A Key Reference To: Laws of Air Pressure

Boyle's Law was first published in 1660 by British chemist Robert Boyle (1627–1691). The law states that at a constant temperature, the volume occupied by a gas is inversely proportional to the pressure applied on the gas. For example, when the pressure applied on a given volume of air is doubled, the air shrinks to half its volume. In other words, air under pressure becomes compressed. Boyle is also noted for his invention of two of the earliest types of **barometer:** the water barometer and the siphon barometer (for more information on barometers, see "Forecasting," page 395).

The companion to Boyle's Law is Charles' Law (also called Gay-Lussac's Law). This 1802 finding by French physicist Jacques Alexandre César Charles (1746–1823) and French chemist Joseph-Louis Gay-Lussac (1778–1850) states that at a constant pressure, the volume of a gas is proportional to the temperature of the gas. This means that as heat is applied to a sample of air, the air expands, and as heat is taken away, the air contracts. Gay-Lussac, incidentally, set a record for height in a hot-air balloon flight in 1804, of over 4 miles (6 kilometers) above ground. His record remained unbroken for the next fifty years.

You can also alter air pressure by adding air to, or removing it from, a closed container, such as a bicycle tire. Each time you drive down the plunger on a bicycle pump, you are squeezing more air molecules into the same volume of space. With each movement of the plunger, air pushes out against the inside of the tire, and the tire feels hard. If you were to continue pumping long enough, the air pressure would increase to the point where the tire would explode.

AIR PRESSURE CHANGES WITH ALTITUDE

Measurements of air pressure may be given in a variety of units.

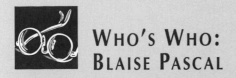

Who's Who: Blaise Pascal

French mathematician and philosopher Blaise Pascal was the first person to explain the connection between air pressure and altitude. He hypothesized that the weight of the atmosphere above Earth's surface is responsible for air pressure at the surface and, by extension, that air pressure decreases as elevation increases.

To test his hypothesis, Pascal conducted an experiment using the newly invented barometer. He took barometer readings at the base and the peak of a mountain. He found that he was correct. The air pressure measured 935 millibars (mb) at ground level and only 828 mb at the mountaintop.

The unit most commonly used by meteorologists is the millibar (mb). The unit of air pressure in the English system is pounds per square inch (psi). At sea level air pressure is equal to about 1,000 mb, or 14.7 psi. Atmospheric pressure decreases with higher altitudes. At about 1,000 feet (300 meters) above sea level, air pressure is about 900 mb (14.1 psi). And if you travel 4 miles (6 kilometers) above the ground, the point at which half of the atmosphere's mass is above and half is below you, the air pressure is about 500 mb (7.3 psi).

Air molecules are constantly bombarding us from all directions, exerting a constant pressure of about 1,000 mb (14.7 psi) at sea level. You may say, "Hold on, I don't feel anything hitting me!" The primary reason for this belief is that the air pressure inside your body balances that outside it. The only way you can notice air pressure is if it changes rapidly, such as when you ascend or descend in an airplane or drive on a steep mountain road. In those cases, the air pressure around you changes more quickly than does the air pressure in you ears and sinuses.

Anyone who has flown on an airplane has experienced the "popping" of his or her ears during take-off and landing. This "popping" is the body's attempt to equalize the pressure imbalance by releasing air from the eustachian tube (the passage connecting the eardrum and the throat).

HIGH-PRESSURE AND LOW-PRESSURE SYSTEMS

Altitude is not the only factor associated with differences in air pressure. Air pressure also differs from location to location on the ground and even from one hour to the next at a single location. It is these changes at ground level that are connected with weather patterns. Even a very small difference in air pressure between two points can signal profound changes in the weather.

Television weather forecasters regularly refer to systems of high pressure and low pressure. There is no set definition of a "high" or "low" pressure system: they are only defined relative to one another. For example, if one area has an air pressure of 1,000 mb (14.5 psi) and a second area has an air pressure of 1,034 mb (15 psi), the former is considered a "low-pressure" area and the latter, a "high-pressure" area.

High- and low-pressure systems are the result of **air masses** of different temperature and moisture content entering and leaving an area. In the **middle latitudes,** which includes the United States, this parade of air masses is nearly constant (see the section on air masses, page 33). As one air mass is replaced by another, the air pressure rises or falls and the weather changes.

High-pressure systems are usually associated with clear skies and low-pressure systems with clouds and **precipitation.** These are only generalities and, due to the interaction of other factors in the atmosphere, do not always hold true. To understand how pressure systems affect the weather, it is necessary to combine the concepts of **convection** and air pressure.

We learned in the discussion of convection that as air is heated, it rises. It leaves in its wake an area of low pressure. One consequence of rising air (and hence a low-pressure area) is that it causes water vapor in the air to condense and form clouds.

Clouds form over low-pressure areas because cool air can hold less water than warm air. The warm air carries water vapor upward until it reaches the **dew point.** This is the temperature at which air can no longer hold water in the vapor state, and the water begins to condense into clouds.

When heavier, colder air from above sinks to fill the space vacated by the warm air, it forms a high-pressure area. The cold air becomes warmer as it falls. This causes water and ice in the clouds to dissolve and the clouds themselves to thin or evaporate entirely, leaving only clear, sunny skies.

WIND: AIR IN MOTION

Wind is the natural movement of air. Winds are produced and acted upon by numerous forces. Among these are **air pressure** differences, Earth's rotation, and friction. Essentially, air attempts to flow from areas of high pressure to areas of low pressure, but is prevented from traveling along such a path directly because of Earth's rotation. And wind speed, although largely a function of pressure differences, is also influenced by Earth's surface features.

PRESSURE CHANGES PRODUCE WINDS

To simplify the discussion of winds, we'll begin by looking at a single factor: the flow of air across a pressure differential. A pressure differential or **pressure gradient** is the difference in atmospheric pressure at any two given locations. The movement of air from a high-pressure to a low-pressure area is the atmosphere's attempt to equalize differences in pressure. When the pressure between the two areas is equalized, the wind stops blowing.

Two main factors determine how fast the wind moves: the difference in air pressure and the distance between two areas. Either a greater pressure differential or a smaller distance between the areas makes for a stronger wind. And, conversely, either a smaller pressure differential or a greater distance between the two areas makes for a weaker wind.

These two factors taken together are called the **pressure gradient force** (PGF). To illustrate this concept, if you have a pressure gradient of 10 mb between two locations set 1,000 kilometers apart, the pressure gradient force is 10 mb/1,000 km = 0.01mb/km. Still air will accelerate to 80 mph (130 kph) in three hours. However, if you take the same pressure gradient yet increase the distance between the two locations to 1,000 miles (400 kilometers), you will find that the wind accelerates to only 40 mph (65 kph) after three hours.

FRICTION SLOWS THE WINDS

Topography (the physical features of land) doesn't produce winds, but it does affect wind speed. As wind blows across a pressure differential, it encounters hills, trees, tall buildings, sand dunes, and other objects that create friction and slow it down. Relatively flat surfaces—such as water, prairies, and deserts—exert little friction on the wind. Over flat terrain, winds reach greater speeds than they do over hilly terrain. Any farmer will tell you that planting a row of trees on otherwise flat land goes a long way toward preventing soil erosion caused by strong winds.

EARTH'S ROTATION CURVES THE WINDS

Imagine a wind blowing from north to south because of a pressure differential between two areas. If the space between the two areas were perfectly flat, one might expect the wind to blow in a perfectly north-south direction. But such is not the case. Instead, the wind is diverted slightly because of an effect known as the **Coriolis effect.** The effect is named for the French scientist Gustave-Gaspard de Coriolis. De Coriolis used mathematical formulas to explain that the path of any object set in motion above a rotating surface will curve in relation to any object on that surface.

To an observer beyond Earth, say on a space shuttle, the wind would not appear to curve—it would blow in a straight line while Earth spun beneath it. But relative to observers on Earth—that is to say, all of us—the wind does appear to curve. One way to understand the Coriolis effect is to think of a person riding on a carousel who throws a ball straight up into the air. When the ball comes down, it lands behind the person who threw it. To the person on the carousel, it seems that the ball's path has curved backwards. However, to a person standing next to the carousel the ball appears to have traveled in a straight vertical path while the carousel rotated beneath it. If we relate this example to Earth, then we are all on the carousel and the wind (as the ball) appears to curve as it travels.

The Coriolis effect influences the direction of winds as follows: In the **Northern Hemisphere** it curves them to the right. In the **Southern Hemisphere** it curves them to the left (see Figure 4).

The Coriolis effect is felt most strongly at the poles. It does not exist at all at the equator, where opposing forces (the turn to the right and the turn to the left) are canceled out.

Gustave-Gaspard de Coriolis.

Putting It all Together

When you combine the forces of pressure gradient and Coriolis effect, you find some very complex global wind patterns. In the Northern Hemisphere, winds spiral clockwise around high-pressure systems (where air is falling) and counter-clockwise around low-pressure systems (where air is rising). In the Southern Hemisphere, the opposite is true. What causes the wind to move like this?

The spiral pattern represents the path of equilibrium between opposing forces. To illustrate this point, imagine you are watching a hot air balloon that's being carried along by the wind (as illustrated in Figure 5). [Note that this example only applies to the Northern Hemisphere. The Coriolis effect works in reverse in the Southern Hemisphere.] At the start of its journey, the balloon is pushed away from a high-pressure system. It moves into a low-pressure system, which is characterized by rising, warm air. Yet, rather than following a straight line into the center of the system, the balloon is pushed to the right by the Coriolis effect.

It is now caught in a tug-of-war between forces pushing it toward the low-pressure system and those pushing it to the right. The balloon finds and settles into a pattern where these two forces are in balance. As it moves from point A to point B to point C and so on, it's simultaneously driven in toward the low-pressure system and to the right. What you find when you connect the points of equilibrium between these forces is a circular path, running counterclockwise around the low pressure area.

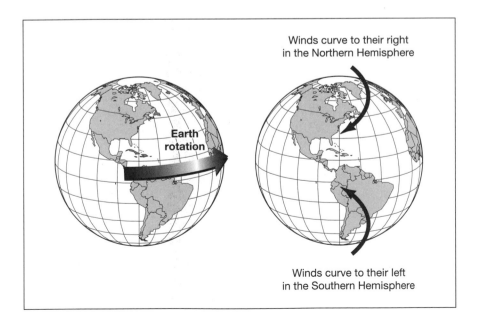

Winds curve to their right
in the Northern Hemisphere

Earth
rotation

Winds curve to their left
in the Southern Hemisphere

Figure 4:
The Coriolis effect.

Now consider the opposite case, where the balloon is swept into the descending, cold air of a high-pressure system. This time, the balloon is simultaneously being pushed away by the high-pressure system and being tugged to the right by the Coriolis effect. The balloon travels to the point where these two forces are in balance. You'll find that the path of equilibrium around a high-pressure system runs clockwise.

One more factor is necessary to complete the description of how the wind travels: friction. Friction causes wind near the ground to behave differently than wind at higher altitudes. The reason is that winds near the ground are slowed down, lessening the Coriolis effect. In fact, for wind blowing toward a low-pressure system just above the ground, the Coriolis effect is so weak that the wind blows right into the low-pressure area. Wind blowing toward that same system in the upper air, due to the Coriolis effect (unimpeded by friction), would circle around the system, as described above.

GLOBAL WIND PATTERNS

At the beginning of this section, we explained that the sun heats Earth unevenly and that the atmosphere strives to even out heat distribution. (Winds are responsible for about two-thirds of the world's heat distribution and **ocean current**s for about one-third of the burden.) In general, winds move between the equator and the poles, bringing warm air to cold areas and cold air to warm areas. Global wind patterns are made

Figure 5: Winds acting on a hot air balloon.

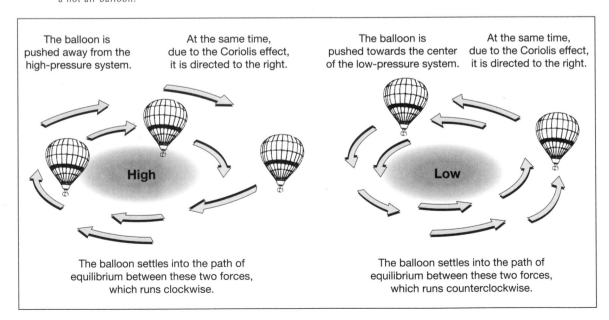

A KEY REFERENCE TO:
BUYS BALLOT'S LAW OF AIR PRESSURE

Dutch meteorologist Christoph Buys Ballot (1817–1890) demonstrated that it's possible, from the direction of the wind, to determine the positions of high- and low-pressure areas. For **winds aloft,** at about the height of low clouds, this is a straightforward equation. For surface winds, however, the angle at which the wind flows is affected by friction due to surface features.

According to the Buys Ballot Law, if you stand with your back to the winds aloft in the Northern Hemisphere, the lower-pressure area is on your left and the high-pressure area is on your right. In the Southern Hemisphere the opposite is true.

more complex by a number of factors, such as Earth's rotation and the locations of land and sea. We will discuss the second factor toward the end of this chapter, on page 67. As you can see in Figure 6 on page 24, the result is a complex pattern of swirling winds, encircling the globe. And these wind patterns are what create the variety of weather conditions at specific regions north and south of the equator.

The global motion of the winds begins with the flow of warm air from the equator to the poles. The air doesn't travel all the way to the poles in one interrupted journey, however. It travels through a series of loops in which warm air rises and cold air falls at different **latitudes.** It is also important to note that, due to the Coriolis effect, these winds do not travel due north or south, but between points southwest and northeast in the Northern Hemisphere and between points northwest and southeast in the Southern Hemisphere. Remember that the Coriolis effect acts differently in the Northern and Southern hemispheres. In the following discussion, examples are given only for the Northern Hemisphere. You can assume that the opposite is true in each example for the Southern Hemisphere.

HADLEY CELLS. The first of these loops, which extend from the equator to 30 degrees latitude north and south, are called **Hadley cell**s. They are named for George Hadley, an English scientist who first explained this air flow pattern in 1753. The air that flows through the Hadley cells begins at the equatorial region (from about 10 degrees latitude south to 10 degrees latitude north), also known as the tropics. This area is the warmest region on Earth, because sunlight hits the surface most directly. The air is warmed and rises by the process of **convection.** The upward movement of air creates a low-pressure zone, which produces the clouds and rains for which the tropics are famous.

Warm air continues rising to the top of the **troposphere,** cooling as it goes. Then it begins to spread out toward the poles. At approximately 30 degrees latitude north and south the air sinks to the surface, warming as it descends. The latitudes at which air rises and falls, marking the boundaries of the cells, are only approximations and shift throughout the year.

High-pressure systems are created in these regions, meaning that skies are generally clear and little **precipitation** occurs. It stands to reason that 30 degrees north and south are the latitudes at which most of the world's deserts are located.

Air descending at these latitudes displaces air at the surface. Most of the displaced air moves back toward the low-pressure belt at the equatorial zone, forming the **trade winds.** Northern- and Southern-hemisphere trade winds meet at **heat equator,** the warmest part of the equatorial zone. The location of the heat equator is generally north of the geographic equator, due to the greater mass of land in the Northern Hemisphere, and it shifts north-to-south with the changing seasons.

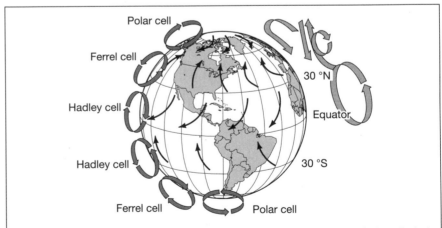

Idealized pattern of circulation of global winds. Note that the actual circulation of winds around the Earth is more complex due to the distribution of land and sea. The left side of this diagram shows the cells through which warm air rises and cold air falls at different latitudes. The right side of the diagram gives a more accurate representation of the vertical motion of winds through these cells.

Figure 6:
Global wind patterns.

A Key Reference To:
How the Horse Latitudes and Doldrums Got Their Names

Horse latitudes and **doldrums** are colorful terms used to describe two regions of Earth at which the winds are nearly still. The horse latitudes are a high-pressure belt that exists at around 30 degrees north and south of the equator. It is in this region that air from the upper troposphere descends to Earth's surface, bringing clear skies.

While sunshine does not create a problem for sailors, the lack of wind does. Many ships over time have become stalled in the horse latitudes. When food would run low, the first to forego feedings were the horses on board. They often were slaughtered to feed the crew or simply thrown overboard. The preponderance of horse corpses floating in the waters throughout this region led to the name "horse latitudes."

The doldrums, an old English word for "dull," is another name for the intertropical convergence zone. This is the zone near the equator where the trade winds coming from north and south meet and nearly cancel each other out. The warm tropical air, rather than traveling horizontally (and creating wind) rises straight up. So-named by sailors stranded in this part of the world, the doldrums is known for its warm, rainy, and still conditions.

Where the trade winds meet they form a broad band of light, variable east-west winds. This area, which is generally cloudy and rainy, is called the **doldrums.** Another name for this region is the **intertropical convergence zone (ITCZ).**

Ferrel cells. Ferrel cells encompass the next wind cycle, in which equatorial air moves one step closer to the poles. These cells are named for American meteorologist William Ferrel, who first described them in 1856. The Ferrel cells cover the region of the globe from about 30 to 60 degrees latitude, north and south, in other words, the temperate regions.

The Ferrel cells begin where the Hadley cells leave off, with the air that falls at 30 degrees latitude. Some of this air, rather than returning to the equator, continues in the direction of the poles. The winds traveling to the poles generally come from the southwest and are curved to the northeast (in the Northern Hemisphere) by the Coriolis effect. For this reason, they are called **westerlies.** At around 60 degrees latitude north and south the westerlies encounter cold polar air. The points where this occurs are called the **polar front**s.

The contrast in temperature between these air masses causes the warmer air to rise. This results in a low-pressure system, bringing clouds and precipitation to regions such as southern Alaska and central Canada. The air that rises forms a circulation pattern called the **upper-air westerlies.** These winds, which flow from west-to-east, are responsible for driving most of the weather systems of the **middle latitudes.** These winds travel in waves that carry warm air poleward and cold air toward the equator.

POLAR CELLS. The final leg of the trek bringing warm air from the equator to the poles takes place within the **polar cell**s. These cells extend from the poles, to 60 degrees latitude north and south.

Some of the warmer air (relative to the cold polar air) rising at the sixtieth parallels heads to the poles. It cools drastically along the way. Once this air reaches a pole, it descends, forming a high pressure area. The displaced air at the surface then heads south. These cold winds, which head from the northeast to the southwest across the polar regions, are known as the **polar easterlies.**

At around the sixtieth parallel the polar easterlies, which have warmed slightly, meet the westerlies (warmer air coming from the thirtieth parallel). The warm air rises and heads back to the pole, completing the polar cell.

Some heat is lost through every cell between the equator to the poles. This means that the atmosphere's attempt to distribute heat across the planet is only partially successful—the poles remain forever colder than the equator.

GLOBAL PRESSURE PATTERNS

As we just learned, air rises and falls at certain **latitudes** as it makes its way from the equator to the poles and back. On Earth's surface, rising air creates low-pressure areas and falling air creates high-pressure areas. These major pressure areas exist along the boundaries between wind cells.

The highs are located around 30 degrees latitude north and south and at the poles, where cold air descends, and the lows are around the equator and 60 degrees north and south, where warm air rises.

It's important to distinguish the major pressure areas encircling the globe from the minor ones responsible for our day-to-day weather. The major high- and low-pressure areas, caused by global wind circulation, cover thousands of square miles each and can persist for months or longer. Small, localized high- and low-pressure areas form and die out in a matter of hours or days.

The world's major high- and low-pressure areas undergo significant shifts north and south with the seasons. They move to the north when it's summer in the **Northern Hemisphere** and to the south when it's winter in the Northern Hemisphere. However, four large pressure areas—two high and two low—maintain their basic position throughout the year. These systems are called **semipermanent highs and lows.** They are called "semipermanent" because they undergo changes in strength, as well as slight shifts in position, throughout the year.

The semipermanent systems are all located in the Northern Hemisphere. The reason for this arrangement is that the **Southern Hemisphere** has far less land mass than the Northern Hemisphere overall, and has virtually no land between 50 degrees latitude and Antarctica. And it is the contrast in temperature of land and sea that results in changes in air pressure. Thus, the Southern Hemisphere has a fairly continuous low-pressure belt running across the globe at around 60 degrees latitude. In contrast, the Northern Hemisphere, due to the positions of land masses, has areas of great temperature contrast at this latitude. In the sub-tropical region, at around 30 degrees latitude south, the Southern Hemisphere has a series of well-defined but shifting high-pressure areas.

The semipermanent highs and lows are called the Aleutian Low, Icelandic Low, Pacific High, and Azores-Bermuda High. In general, the lows produce storms and the highs influence the direction in which the storms travel. We will now examine each semipermanent high and low in greater detail.

ALEUTIAN LOW. The Aleutian Low is a huge low-pressure system over the north Pacific Ocean, centered between Alaska and eastern Siberia. It lies above tiny land masses called the Aleutian Islands, from which it gets its name. The Aleutian Low is created by the collision of cold polar air and warm, moist Pacific air. It is much stronger in winter, when temperature contrasts are greatest, than it is in summer. The Aleutian Low churns out the bulk of the world's **cyclone**s, whirling, low-pressure systems that give rise to storms. Canada and the northwestern United States are prime recipients of Aleutian-generated storms.

ICELANDIC LOW. The Icelandic Low system is located over the north Atlantic Ocean, Iceland, and southern Greenland. While it is a weaker system than the Aleutian Low in winter, it is the stronger of the two in summer. The primary effect of the Icelandic Low is to intercept cyclones that have traveled across North America, strengthen them, and redirect them toward western Europe.

PACIFIC HIGH. The Pacific High covers a large area over the Pacific Ocean, northeast of Hawaii. Storms coming from the Far East are deflected northward by the Pacific High, in the direction of the Aleutian Low.

AZORES-BERMUDA HIGH. The Azores-Bermuda High occupies a huge area in the east Atlantic Ocean, between the eastern coast of North America and the western coast of Europe. It changes in size throughout the year. When it is large, it strongly repels all storms that come its way. Even the strongest **hurricane**s, generated in the band of warm waters running from the south of Florida eastward to northern Africa, are bent around this system. As a hurricane heads north, it encounters the large high-pressure system and is forced westward through the Caribbean and toward the eastern seaboard of the United States. (For more information on the paths of hurricanes, see "Hurricanes," page 273.)

UPPER-AIR WINDS

Earlier in this section we learned about the three main types of surface winds that blow between the equator to the poles—**trade winds, westerlies,** and **polar easterlies**—and the major pressure systems that generate and steer surface winds. The winds that blow in the middle and upper levels of the troposphere, also known as **winds aloft** take on a different pattern.

In general, the winds aloft run in the opposite direction from surface winds. For example, the surface trade winds blow toward the equator from the northeast to the southwest (in the Northern Hemisphere) and the upper-air trade winds blow back to the sub-tropics (30 degrees latitude) from southwest to northeast.

UPPER-AIR WESTERLIES. In the middle latitudes, however, the winds circulate in a different pattern: they move in wave-like patterns, from west to east. Where these waves crest to the north they form **ridge**s, and when they dip to the south they form **trough**s (see Figure 7.) It is essential to understand the flow of **upper-air westerlies** since they have a very significant impact on the weather of the United States and Canada.

These waves, through a series of ridges and troughs, cycle warm **air mass**es northward and cold air masses southward. From the base of a trough, the southerly winds blow warm air masses northward. And from the top of a ridge, northerly winds blow cold air masses southward. The net result is that upper-air westerlies transfer heat toward the poles and cold air toward the equator.

In addition to cycling warm and cold air, upper-air westerlies transport high- and low-pressure systems from west to east. These pressure systems exist within the ridges and troughs. To illustrate this, draw an upside-down "U," representing a ridge. Draw a series of arrows along the sides and top, from left to right, marking the flow of the upper-air westerlies. Then draw an "H" in the center. This is the position of a high-pressure system, within which winds blow in a clockwise direction. Now

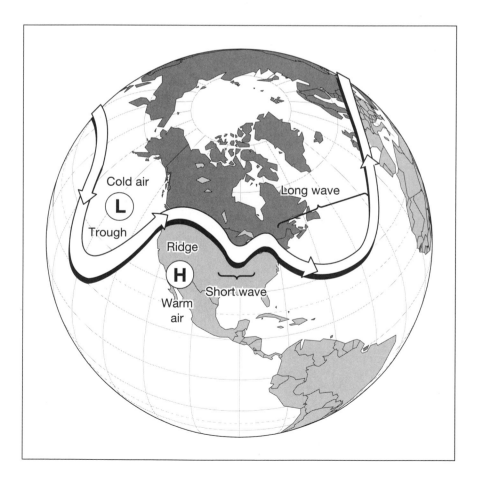

Figure 7:
Upper-air westerlies.

draw a rightside-up "U" to represent a trough. Draw an "L" in the center to mark the position of the low-pressure system, within which winds blow in a counterclockwise direction. As the wave moves eastward, the highs and lows in the winds aloft is further explained in the section on convergence and divergence (see page 32).

In the upper half of the **troposphere,** the entire hemisphere is encircled at any given time by just two to five waves of upper-air westerlies. These long waves are called **Rossby waves** after Carl G. Rossby, the Swedish-American meteorologist who first discovered them. The waves are called "long waves" because the distance between adjacent troughs ranges from about 2,500 to 5,000 miles (4,000 to 8,000 kilometers). When Rossby waves change in length (the distance from one trough to the next) or amplitude (the distance north-to-south they cover), they produce changes in the weather beneath them.

The flow of Rossby waves ranges between two extremes: from a nearly straight line west-to-east to a nearly continuous north-south pattern with deep troughs and steep ridges. In the former case, Rossby waves primarily carry moist Pacific air eastward, bringing mild and fair weather to much of the United States. In the latter case, great contrasts in temperature are produced by cold air being pulled south and warm air being pushed north. Warm and cold air masses collide, initiating storm systems (for more information, see the sections on fronts and storms, pages 37 and 41). Rossby waves can shift back and forth between these extremes rapidly, even within a single day.

Within the Rossby waves are ripples, called **short waves.** The name might be misleading. Although they are shorter than Rossby waves, the short waves are still quite long. They generally have a wavelength of a few hundred miles. It takes only about twelve of them to encircle the hemisphere. Whereas Rossby waves are responsible for the formation and steering of large-scale weather patterns, the short waves add strength to developing storm systems. They influence the speed of winds and amount of precipitation associated with a storm. The short waves travel at much faster speeds than do their longer counterparts.

JET STREAMS. The world's fastest upper-air winds are imbedded within westerlies as well as within subtropical winds aloft. They are called **jet streams.** Jet streams are narrow bands of wind that blow through the top of the troposphere in a west-to-east direction. Their average speed is about 60 mph (100 kph), but they often exceed 120 mph (200

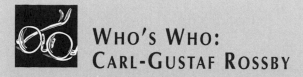

WHO'S WHO: CARL-GUSTAF ROSSBY

Swedish-born meteorologist Carl-Gustaf Rossby (1898–1957) chose to enter to relatively primitive field of meteorology after studying mathematics and a number of scientific disciplines in college. He first worked for a handful of geophysical and meteorological institutes throughout Europe before coming to work for the U.S. Weather Bureau in 1926.

Although his ideas about the influence of upper atmospheric winds on weather conditions were initially shunned by conservative directors at the Bureau, Rossby soon made a name for himself. His research focused, in particular, on the wavy motion of upper-air westerlies, now known as Rossby waves. He showed how this air flow drives weather patterns.

Rossby is credited with modernizing the entire field of meteorology. For instance, he developed mathematical and computer forecasting models that greatly improved the ability of meteorologists to make weather predictions. He also identified where jet streams would exist and how they would behave, before they had ever been discovered.

For further reading on Carl Rossby, see Pine, Devera. "Carl-Gustaf Rossby." *Notable Twentieth-Century Scientists.* Vol. 3. Ed. Emily J. McMurray. Detroit: Gale Research, 1995.

kph). The fastest moving jet streams greatly exceed that value, however, and have been clocked at more than 280 mph (450 kph).

Jet streams occur in regions with the largest differences in air temperature and pressure at high altitudes. In the **middle latitudes** of each hemisphere this region occurs over the **polar front,** where the mild westerlies meet the cold polar easterlies. In the subtropical latitudes of each hemisphere, this region occurs around 30 degrees north and south, where the warm trade winds meet the westerlies.

In either hemisphere, jet streams tend to move faster during winter, than during summer. The reason for this pattern is that a larger temperature differential exists in the winter. For example, in winter it may be

32°F (0°C) in Michigan and 80°F (30°C) in Florida, a difference of almost 50°F (30°C). On a typical day in summer in contrast, it can be about 80°F (25°C) in Michigan and 100°F (37°C) in Florida, a difference of only 20°F (12°C).

In addition, the latitudes at which jet streams travel shift throughout the year. In the winter they are closer to the equator and in the summer, closer to the poles. The reason for this pattern is that during the Northern Hemisphere's winter, cold polar air is swept further south. In the process, the cold air/warm air boundary also moves farther south. Conversely, in the summer, mild air is swept further north and the cold air/warm air boundary moves northward. Note that these northward and southward shifts in cold air/warm air boundaries occur simultaneously in the Southern Hemisphere.

Jet streams are not the only phenomenon to inhabit the boundary between warm air and cold air. Storms also occur in this region. For this reason, weather forecasters consider the path of the jet stream a useful tool in predicting where storms will occur. Jet streams are also reliable indicators of temperature changes. When a jet stream dips southward, it brings with it cold air. And when a jet stream shifts to the north, it brings warmer air in its wake.

CONVERGENCE AND DIVERGENCE

Within a jet stream, winds regularly shift in direction and speed. They alternate between north and south as they pass through the stream's ridges and troughs. They speed up or slow down as they pass in and out of the jet maximum, the fastest region within the jet stream. Any change in wind speed or direction causes air to either pile up or spread out. In the former case, when air moves inward toward a central point, it is called **convergence.** In the latter case, when air moves outward from a central point, it is called **divergence.**

Convergence and divergence are perhaps easier to understand in this example involving traffic patterns. Convergence is when a stream of cars enters an already crowded freeway, causing a slowdown. Divergence is what occurs when a two-lane highway expands to a four-lane highway. Cars spread out between all four lanes and traffic speeds up.

When winds converge at high altitudes, they diverge beneath at the surface. And when winds diverge at high altitudes, they converge beneath at the surface. This is because convergence and divergence affect air pressure over a vertical gradient. Specifically, convergence raises air pressure and divergence lowers air pressure. Thus, when winds diverge aloft, lowering the pressure, surface winds converge to the point beneath the divergence. The surface winds then rush upward to the low-pressure area. The surface winds stop rising when the pressure between points above and below has been equalized.

When we speak of the factors that produce large-scale weather patterns in the middle latitudes, the story starts with convergence and divergence aloft. With the upper-air winds (westerlies and the jet stream), areas of convergence and divergence coincide with ridges and troughs. Winds tend to strengthen as they curve clockwise in ridges and weaken as they curve counterclockwise in troughs. Thus, as winds approach a trough they decrease in speed, converging to the west of a trough. As the wind passes through the trough and heads into a ridge, it curves clockwise and picks up speed. This results in divergence just before entering (to the west of) a ridge.

Let's look at the case of convergence aloft. In the upper air, winds blow toward a central point and pressure builds. The air can't keep on piling up indefinitely, so it looks for an escape. If it's already at the top of the troposphere it can rise no further. Thus, it is forced to travel downward to an area where pressure is lower.

This creates an area of high-pressure on the surface, from which winds flow out in a clockwise direction. In other words, an **anticyclone** is created. The air from above will continue to descend, strengthening the anticyclone, until the pressure at the surface equals the pressure aloft. The air from above warms as it descends, causing the water vapor within it to evaporate. Thus, an anticyclone is associated with clear, settled weather conditions.

Now take the opposite case, where winds aloft are diverging. The air below travels upward toward this area of low pressure, leaving a surface area of low pressure in its wake. A convergence forms on the surface, where air rushes counterclockwise into the center of this surface low and rises. As the rising air cools, it forms clouds and precipitation.

This system is called a cyclone, also known as a storm. As long as the divergence aloft is stronger than the surface convergence, air will be pulled upward and the cyclone strengthened. Once these two forces come into balance, the storm dies out.

AIR MASSES

An **air mass** is one of the few stable elements in the ever-changing world of weather. An air mass is a large quantity of air where temperature and moisture content is fairly consistent throughout. Air masses commonly cover thousands of square miles, the size of several states. Air masses are produced by the heating or cooling effect of the land or water beneath them.

Air masses form when two conditions are met: first, they require a large, relatively homogenous parcel of land or sea; and second, they require stability. That is to say, air must remain undisturbed over the surface while it warms up or cools down to the surface temperature and absorbs moisture (if over a watery surface). It takes an air mass two to three days to form over water and two to three weeks to form over land.

Air masses form primarily over polar and tropical regions. Since the air does not stay still for long over temperate **latitude**s (including the United States), air masses generally do not form over those regions.

An air mass typically hovers above the surface where it was created until set into motion by shifting winds. It will then head off into a different region, introducing its temperature and moisture content to areas through which it travels. For example, a tropical air mass can bring warm, wet weather to the central United States or an arctic air mass can bring cold, dry weather to northern United States and Canada. The East Coast of the United States is one site where several air masses meet, resulting in highly variable weather.

The weather in each part of the world is shaped by the air masses that dominate that region. The weather in a region on any given day is dependent largely on which particular air mass is overhead. Over coastal areas, however, rapidly shifting winds bring a variety of air masses and changing weather. An air mass tends to remain in one place longer over inland areas, bringing relatively stable weather.

When a single air mass remains over a region for an extended period, it produces conditions called **air mass weather.** This pattern occurs in various parts of the United States depending on the time of year. For example, the Southeast can count on hot weather and daily afternoon thunderstorms in the summer and the Pacific Northwest is treated to cold, rainy weather for long periods in the winter.

Each air mass is given a two-letter classification. The first tells whether it has traveled over land or sea and the second refers to its point of origin. The second factor is crucial to determining the mass's moisture content. The first letter of the designation may be "c" for continental, meaning that it has traveled over land and is dry or "m" for maritime, meaning that it has traveled over sea and is moist. The second letter of an air mass's identifier tag may be "P" (polar), "A" (arctic), or "T" (tropical). Some meteorologists do not use a separate designation for arctic air, since arctic air that travels southward becomes warmer and is virtually indistinguishable from polar air.

By combining the two letters of a designation, you describe the temperature and moisture content of an air mass. For instance, the label mT refers to a warm, moist air mass that formed in the tropics and traveled over seas.

In the following section, we will summarize each of the six air mass types: continental arctic, maritime arctic, continental polar, maritime polar, continental tropical, and maritime tropical. Keep in mind that continental air masses are of far less importance in the **Southern Hemisphere,** which has considerably less land mass than the **Northern Hemisphere.**

CONTINENTAL ARCTIC AIR MASS (cA)

This frigid air originating near the North Pole greatly affects the weather of Canada and, to a far lesser degree, the weather of the northern United States. It forms above Greenland, Siberia, northern Alaska, northern Canada, and islands in the Arctic Ocean. The temperature of this dry air can dip as low as -80°F (-61°C) in the winter. For the most part it produces cold, dry conditions. Occasionally it picks up moisture while crossing a body of water and brings snowy weather.

MARITIME ARCTIC AIR MASS (mA)

This air is largely responsible for the cold weather experienced by western Europe. It brings low temperatures in the summer and very low temperatures in the winter. It forms over the ice-covered Arctic region and travels over large bodies of water (such as the northern Atlantic Ocean and Greenland Sea) which warm it somewhat and cause it to absorb more moisture before reaching Europe. These air masses brings rain in the summer and snow in the winter.

Arctic air masses also form over Antarctica, but have virtually no effect on the weather in the Southern Hemisphere. The reason for this pattern is that, except for the very tip of South America, there is little land mass far enough south to feel the impact of antarctic air masses.

CONTINENTAL POLAR AIR MASS (cP)

This type of air mass forms over land in Alaska, northwestern Canada, northern Europe and Siberia. There is no cP air mass in the Southern

Hemisphere because there is little land mass south of 50 degrees latitude. A cP air mass begins as very cold, dry, stable air, and picks up heat and a small amount of moisture (mostly from the Great Lakes) as it travels south over warmer ground. A cP air mass that starts out with a temperature between -40 and -34°F (-40 and -30°C) over Alaska, may warm up to between 20 and 23°F (-5 and -10°C) by the time it reaches Florida.

A cP air mass exhibits greatly different qualities in summer than in winter. In the winter it consists of very cold, dry air, almost as cold as arctic air. It brings low temperatures and clear skies to the north and central United States, and even dips into the southern states on occasion. Its southernmost penetration occurs when much of the United States is covered by snow. Snow reflects incoming sunlight and keeps the ground and air above it colder. In the summer, a cP air mass starts out cool and warms considerably as it travels south.

MARITIME POLAR AIR MASS (mP)

Siberia and the northern Pacific and Atlantic oceans are the points of origin of mP air masses. These air masses start out cold, but not as cold as their continental counterparts. Usually their temperatures hover just above freezing. As they travel south over warmer waters, they become warmer and wetter.

The regions affected most by these air masses are western Europe, southern Australia, New Zealand, the extreme southern Pacific Ocean, and the east and west coasts of North America. Maritime polar air masses bring snow and rain in winter and fog and drizzle in summer. The mP air mass that travels over the Atlantic Ocean brings about the days of dreary weather the East Coast experiences in spring and early summer.

CONTINENTAL TROPICAL AIR MASS (cT)

These air masses build up over desert regions and are the world's hottest. A mass of continental tropical air tends to hover where it was formed, but sometimes moves away. If it hovers over another region for any length of time, it can bring about a drought. As an example, a cT mass may form over the deserts of the southwest United States and then travel to the plains states, where it remains for weeks. A cT air mass picks up moisture as it crosses over lakes and rivers, making it cooler and more humid.

MARITIME TROPICAL AIR MASS (mT)

An mT air mass consists of warm, moist air and forms over tropical and subtropical waters. The mT air masses that invade the eastern United

States begin over the Gulf of Mexico, the Caribbean Sea, and the Atlantic Ocean. Those that affect the western United States form over the Pacific Ocean, from Mexico to Hawaii.

In the summer, mT air masses bring very warm, humid air and rain. Along the Gulf Coast they bring daily thunderstorms. In the winter, mT air is usually prevented by a wall of cold polar air from reaching all but the extreme south of the United States. On the rare occasion when mT air is drawn northward, it brings unseasonably mild weather and clouds. It also brings the rains that wash away the snow, disappointing skiers.

FRONTS: WHERE THE ACTION IS

Air masses are transported around the globe by winds. As one air mass blows into a region, it encounters an air mass that is already there. What occurs next is often described as a battle, since in order to advance, one air mass must push the other out of the way.

The line where two air masses meet is called a **front.** A front is so named because of its similarity to the line where two armies meet in battle (see box, page 38). Fronts can be moving or stationary. When they move it means that one air mass is gaining ground, while another is losing ground. In contrast, a stationary front marks a region of stability between the air masses.

As a front passes through an area, it produces weather conditions ranging from gentle winds and light rains all the way up to violent storms. When a mass of cold air displaces a mass of warm air, it is said that a **cold front** has come through. Conversely, when a cold air mass is displaced by a warm air mass, a **warm front** has come through.

The interaction of warm and cold air masses is most common in the **middle latitudes,** in other words, the temperate regions. Included among these regions are the continental United States and southern Canada in the **Northern Hemisphere** and southern Australia in the **Southern Hemisphere**). The mixing of air with great differences in temperature and pressure produces storms. It is the temperate regions, therefore, that experience some of the world's most violent weather.

WARM FRONTS

A **warm front** is the leading edge of a mass of warm air that overtakes a mass of colder air. The warm air, being less dense, slips over the cold air which hovers close to the ground. The warm air cools as it rises

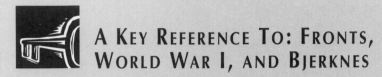

A Key Reference To: Fronts, World War I, and Bjerknes

The term "fronts" was first used during an intensive period of meteorological study in Norway. This period began during World War I, when European nations stopped broadcasting weather reports publicly for fear they would be used by advancing enemy troops. Countries like Norway, which were neutral during the war, were left largely without weather information.

In order to create their own forecasts, Norwegian meteorologists had to improve their understanding of how the weather works. They far exceeded their own goals and ended up creating a science based not only on observations (as it had been up to that point) but on the laws of physics.

From 1918 to 1923 meteorologists from across Scandinavia, led by Norwegian physicist Vilhelm Bjerknes, formed an institute known as the Bergen School. There they collected information, primarily through the use of weather balloons, and discovered the existence of distinct air masses. They also learned that these air masses were transported by the upper winds. Scientists at the Bergen school were most interested in the conditions produced when air masses collide.

Since the war dominated all news of the day, it was natural to explain the behavior of air masses in military terms. The weather-watchers described the middle latitudes as a battleground on which air masses were like armies, each one trying to advance on the other. Bjerknes gave the name "front" to the boundary between air masses, where the battle was taking place.

and the water vapor within it condenses. This results in the formation of wispy clouds at high altitudes.

A warm front has a very gradual slope. In fact, when the leading edge of the air mass is 3,000 feet (1,000 meters) above us, the base can still be more than 100 miles (150 kilometers) away. As the middle level and base of the warm front come in contact with the colder air mass, the warmer air cools and water vapor condenses. This forms layers of clouds at middle and lower altitudes.

As a warm front approaches an area the **air pressure** decreases and **precipitation** begins, sometimes lasting for several days. Fairly strong winds may accompany this precipitation for a day or so when the base of the front sweeps past an area. Once the front passes through, skies generally clear up and temperatures rise.

COLD FRONTS

Cold fronts are more closely associated with violent weather than are warm fronts. When a cold front moves into an area, the cold air (being denser than the existing warm air) wedges underneath the warm air and forces it sharply upward. This occurs because a cold front is very steep. At a distance of only about 30 miles (50 kilometers) behind the leading edge of the air mass, the cold air may reach 3,000 feet (1,000 meters) above ground. The precise steepness of cold front depends on the speed at which it's moving.

The warm air that is forced upward by the cold air mass produces tall clouds, and sometimes **cumulonimbus** (thunderstorm) clouds. These clouds, in turn, bring rain and possibly **thunderstorm**s. The storms are accompanied by strong winds, produced by a drop in pressure created by the rising warm air. Where a cold front advances rapidly, fierce thunderstorms develop in a band called a **squall line.**

Cold fronts tend to pass through an area very quickly, so their effects are harsh but short-lived. The drop in temperature they bring is variable. It ranges from just a few degrees to more than 35°F (10°C). In the summer, a cold front may simply bring drier air into a region, lowering the humidity considerably while barely affecting the temperature. The cold front may leave in its wake a band of clouds which produce rains of lesser intensity than the initial storms, but usually skies clear behind the cold front.

STATIONARY FRONTS

A **stationary front** represents a stand-off between two air masses. It occurs when one air mass pushes against a second air mass and neither side budges.

Stationary fronts often exist in the Canadian Rocky Mountains. There, cold, continental polar air from the east moves westward until it reaches the mountains. At the same time, warmer maritime polar air from the west moves eastward until it also hits the Rockies. Neither air mass moves past the mountains to overtake the other.

If both air masses are relatively dry, then clear to partly cloudy conditions prevail at the front. However, if the warmer air is moist, then some of this air rises above the cold air and forms clouds and, possibly, precipitation.

When one air mass begins to move over or under the other air mass, the front ceases to be stationary. It becomes either a cold front or a warm front, depending on which air mass is advancing and which is retreating.

OCCLUDED FRONTS

The final possible outcome of a meeting between air masses is called an **occluded front** (or "occlusion"). An occluded front is formed by the interaction of three air masses: one cold, one cool, and one warm. The result is a multi-tiered air system, with cold air wedged on the bottom, cool air resting partially on top of the cold air, and warm air pushed up above both colder air masses (see Figure 8).

There are two types of occluded front: cold and warm. **Cold occlusions,** which are much more common than warm ones, occur when a fast-moving cold front overtakes a slower-moving warm front. The cold front thrusts the warm air upward and continues to advance until it encounters cool air. The leading edge of the cold front then noses under the cool air, forcing it upward also.

When a cold occluded front is approaching (but before it reaches an area), the weather is similar to that when a warm front passes through. Clouds form in the upper, middle, and lower layers of the **troposphere**

Figure 8:
An occluded front.

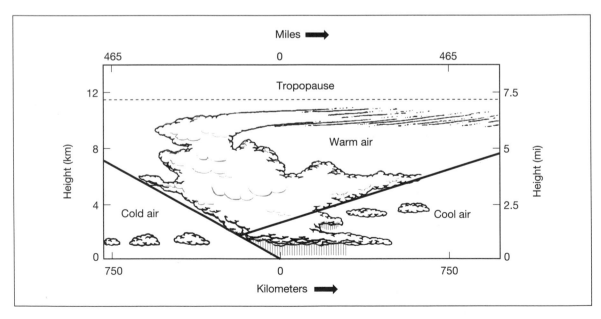

and there is precipitation. As the front passes overhead, however, it is accompanied by stormy weather and a sharp drop in temperature, similar to (but usually not as strong as) that associated with a cold front.

A **warm occlusion** forms under similar conditions as a cold occlusion, except that the cool air mass is the one advancing on the warm air. It pushes the warm air up and runs into cold air. The advancing cool front is then pushed upward, above the cold front. As a warm occluded front passes through an area, it produces weather conditions similar to those produced by an advancing warm front.

WHAT IS A STORM?

The word "storm" has come to represent many different types of weather phenomena. It is most often associated with unsettled weather conditions, such as **heavy rain, thunderstorm**s, and snowstorms. Storms thus defined can be severe, causing floods, damaging homes, and even causing injury or death; or they can be mild, bringing rain or snow but causing little or no damage.

In this section we define storms as large-scale weather systems centered around an area of low atmospheric pressure, drawing in contrasting **warm** and **cold front**s. They produce wind, clouds, **precipitation,** and the types of unsettled weather listed above, and cover hundreds to thousands of square kilometers. In a global sense, storms are a major mechanism of air circulation, pushing cold air southward and warm air northward.

Another word for a large-scale storm is a **cyclone.** A cyclone is a weather system in which winds spiral counterclockwise in the **Northern Hemisphere** and clockwise in the **Southern Hemisphere,** around a low-pressure area. The technical name for the kind of storm system that sweeps through the middle latitudes is an **extratropical cyclone** (or "midlatitude cyclone"). This term literally means a cyclone that is formed outside of the tropics. It differs from a **tropical cyclone,** one formed in the tropics, in that tropical cyclones are storms that don't involve **front**s. While **tornado**es and hurricanes are sometimes called cyclones, it should be noted that these are particular kinds of cyclones.

CONDITIONS RIPE FOR STORMS

The formation and sustenance of an extratropical cyclone requires vast amounts of energy. This energy is generated by the contrast between cold air and warm air. Temperature contrasts are particularly strong along fronts, and that is where cyclones are generally found. Occasionally, extratropical cyclones are formed in the absence of fronts. In such cases, contrasts in air temperature within a single air mass are produced as the air mass travels across warm and cold surfaces and is heated unevenly.

The birth of an extratropical cyclone also depends on conditions in the upper atmosphere. Specifically, an area of horizontal **divergence** is required. The divergence of winds aloft reduces the pressure at the top of a vertical column of air. Air from below ascends to this low-pressure area aloft, creating a surface area of low pressure. This, in turn, results in the **convergence** of both cold air and warm air at the center of the surface low. The contrasting air temperatures enhance the **pressure gradient,** causing the winds to blow faster. The process of **cyclogenesis** has begun.

CYCLOGENESIS: THE BIRTH OF A CYCLONE

As air converges to the center of the surface low-pressure area, warm air rises over cold air. The warm air cools as it rises and the vapor within it begins to condense and form clouds. With the transformation of water vapor into liquid water comes a release of **latent heat,** which also provides energy to the storm system.

The heavy, cold air then slides beneath the rising warm air and noses further into the warm front. As a result, it pushes more warm air upward. The winds spiral in a counter-clockwise fashion (in the Northern Hemisphere) and the fronts rotate. (Return to the section on winds, page 19, for an explanation of why winds blow counter-clockwise around a low-pressure system in the Northern Hemisphere). The greater the contrast between temperatures of the fronts, the greater the pressure differential. And the greater the pressure differential between the center of the storm and the surrounding air, the faster the winds blow.

Another force that affects the cyclone's wind speed is the **conservation of angular momentum.** This scientific law states that as the radius of a spinning object decreases, its speed increases, and as its radius increases, its speed decreases. For example, think of a figure skater spinning on the ice. When she places her arms straight over her head, she spins faster. And when she stretches her arms out to her sides, she spins more slowly.

Similarly, the speed at which a cyclone turns is related to how tightly wrapped the winds are about its center. As winds blow into the center of the low-pressure system, they spiral more and more tightly. However, if the storm center is forced to expand, the winds spin more slowly and the storm loses intensity.

Such an explanation occurs when a storm system crosses over a mountain. Above a mountaintop, there is less distance between Earth's surface and the top of the troposphere than there is at lower altitudes. Over a mountain, the storm becomes compacted into a smaller vertical space. It becomes flattened from a tall, skinny shape into a short, fat shape with a larger radius. This causes the winds to blow more slowly and the storm to lose intensity. When the storm passes beyond the mountain, it has more room to stretch out vertically. The winds then spin faster and the storm regains intensity.

TRACING THE PATH OF A STORM

The paths that storms follow shift throughout the year, as the boundaries between cold air and warm air shift. As warm air covers more

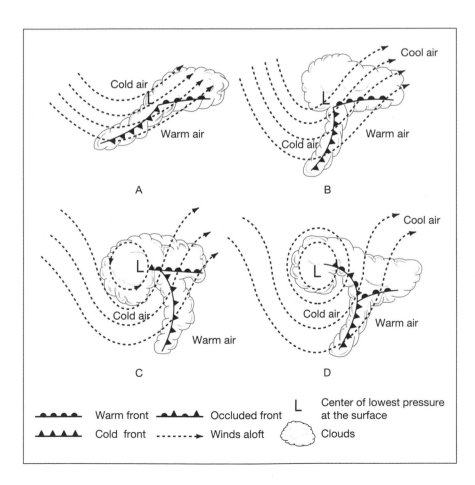

Figure 9: Cyclogenesis. A. Cold air and warm air converge toward the center of the surface low. B. The cold front advances, forcing the warm air upward. The water vapor within the warm air condenses and forms clouds. C. The winds blow faster and the storm intensifies. D. An occluded front is formed and the storm begins to die out.

of the Northern Hemisphere in summer, this boundary shifts to the north, through Canada and the northern United States. And as cold air makes its way southward in winter, the boundary shifts accordingly, running through the central and southern states. Storms tend to follow these boundaries, since they feed on contrasting warm and cold air.

WEATHER CONDITIONS ALONG A STORM'S PATH

A storm generally involves three air masses: one cold, one warm, and one cool. This is the pattern one finds in the formation of an **occluded front.** As air masses move from west to east, the cold front is to the west and nudges along the warm air, which, in turn, butts up against the cool air to the east. The air masses cover huge north-south areas, often running from the northern edge to the southern edge of the United States. Thus, the same storm system can affect the weather across the entire country.

Weather conditions look quite different on either side of the storm. Locations ahead of (to the east of) the storm experience a high layer of thin clouds which grow thicker as the warm front approaches. And for locations to the west, where the cold front has already passed through and the storm is over, clear skies and chilly air remain.

Weather Service International Corporation's STORMcast® image, which tracks and predicts the paths of severe local storms as they happen.

Now let's look at conditions for locations where the storm is overhead. As the steep cold front advances, it forces the warm air up sharply. This powerful **convection** produces tall clouds that often give rise to thunderstorms and possibly even tornadoes, all along the cold front. At the same time, 625 miles (1,000 kilometers) to the east, the warm front passes through. The gentle slope of the warm front noses upward, over the cool air. This produces clouds and light rain. Between the cold and the warm front is a pocket of warm air. That area experiences warm temperatures and hazy or clear skies.

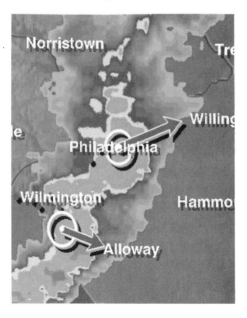

As the whole system moves eastward over the next few days, the cold front out paces the warm front. As a result, the pocket of warm air between the cold and cool air grows smaller and smaller. When the cold air finally meets the cool air, the warm air is forced completely off the surface. An occluded front is thus formed and the storm begins to die out. Rain and clouds at the occluded front can persist for days.

ANTICYCLONES

An **anticyclone,** or high-pressure area, typically follows on the trail of a cyclone. The anticyclone strengthens the cyclone by providing a contrast in pressure with the cyclone's low. It is also brings about the calm, clear weather we see once a storm passes.

Anticyclones are the opposite of cyclones in every respect. They are centers of high pressure from which winds flow outward in a clockwise (in the Northern Hemisphere) pattern. Anticyclones form when there is a convergence of air above. That air descends, forming a high-pressure area on the surface, from which winds diverge.

Because clouds and water droplets in the air **evaporate** as the descending air warms, anticyclones usually bring about clear skies. And while cyclones are associated with competing fronts, anticyclones favor the formation and sustenance of a single, uniform air mass.

WATER IN THE AIR

Water plays an important role in the creation of all weather conditions. Some concentration of water always exists in the air, even on sunny days. When that concentration is so great that the air can hold no more water vapor, the water begins to condense (enter the liquid phase). **Condensation** may take the form of clouds, **fog, dew,** or **frost.** When water (or ice) in the clouds aggregates into units that are large enough, they fall to the ground as rain or snow.

In this section and in the sections that follow we'll study how water shifts between the phases of gas, liquid and solid and what its weather-making role is in each phase.

HOW WATER BECOMES A GAS

Water molecules are always in motion. The speed with which they move is a function of temperature. That is, a function of their average **kinetic energy.**

When they possess very little heat, water molecules are nearly still. The molecules are drawn together by their opposing electrical charges into the hexagonal (six-sided) crystalline configuration of ice. Except for slight vibrations, frozen molecules cease to move.

As heat is added to the ice, the molecules begin to move more rapidly. With the addition of enough heat, the molecules move fast

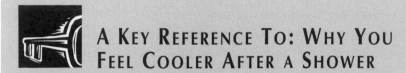

A KEY REFERENCE TO: WHY YOU FEEL COOLER AFTER A SHOWER

Have you ever wondered why your skin feels cool after showering or taking a swim? Before you dry off you may find your skin covered with goosebumps, even when it's hot outside! The goosebumps are caused by the evaporation of water from your skin.

The process of evaporation requires energy called **latent heat.** This type of heat does not raise the water's temperature, but makes possible the conversion of water from one phase to another. When water evaporates from your body it takes away latent heat, which makes your skin feel cooler.

enough to break the bonds of the ice structure. The result is that ice melts and becomes liquid water.

The molecules in liquid water are still connected to one another, although not in the rigid configuration of ice. They remain linked because there is an electrical attraction between oxygen atoms and hydrogen atoms in different molecules.

With the addition of more heat, the molecules in liquid water move even faster. The molecules at the surface eventually move fast enough to overcome the electrical attractions connecting them to other molecules. Those molecules break free, leaving the liquid water and entering the air as a gas.

The process by which water changes from a liquid to a gas is called **evaporation.** Evaporation occurs naturally from any body of water. For example, water evaporates from a lake when the lake is heated by the sun. When water molecules enter the gaseous phase, they retain the heat they absorbed in the liquid, the heat they required to break free. Thus, evaporation takes heat away from water and adds it to the air.

ABSOLUTE HUMIDITY

Absolute humidity is a measure of the amount of water vapor in the air. It is expressed as the mass of water per unit volume of air. For instance, the absolute humidity on a given day may be .5 cubic inches (25 grams) of water per cubic yard of air. There is a limit as to how much

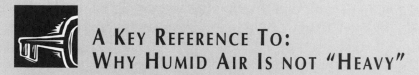

A Key Reference To: Why Humid Air Is not "Heavy"

It is a common misconception that humid air is "heavy." In reality, humid air is less dense, and lighter, than dry air at the same temperature and pressure. The reason is that water molecules are lighter than oxygen and nitrogen, two other molecules present in air. And for every molecule of water that enters a parcel of air, oxygen and nitrogen molecules are displaced. The net result is that when humidity increases, the air becomes less dense.

The reason that humid air feels heavier than dry air is that humidity makes us feel hotter on hot days. When the humidity is low, sweat evaporates more quickly. And our bodies are cooled as sweat evaporates. However, on a hot humid day, although our sweat glands continue to perspire, the sweat evaporates much more slowly. It remains on our skin, making us feel weighted down and hot.

water vapor can exist within a given volume of air at any given temperature. That limit is called the **saturation point.** For example, if you fill a cup of water half-way and seal the top with plastic wrap, the air in the top-half of the cup will soon reach the saturation point. After that, water molecules will evaporate from the water's surface and condense back into it, at the same rate.

The saturation point is a function of air temperature. The warmer the air, the more water it can hold, and the higher the saturation point. For example, at about 50°F (10°C), a cubic yard of air can hold about .5 cubic inches (9 grams) of water vapor. At about 75°F (about 25°C), the same parcel of air can hold an entire cubic inch (.061 cubic centimeters) of water. And at 100°F (38°C), a cubic yard of air can hold 2 cubic inches (.122 cubic centimeters) of water.

Another factor affecting saturation is air flow. On a still day, air remains in place and becomes **saturated** relatively quickly. However, on a windy day, air reaches the saturation point more slowly. The reason is that when there is wind, the humid air is blown away and the water vapor goes with it. As drier air moves in, more water molecules can evaporate

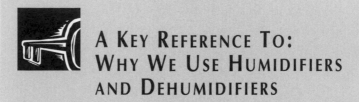

A Key Reference To: Why We Use Humidifiers and Dehumidifiers

Have you ever wondered why the air in your home feels so dry in the winter? Or why your basement gets damp in the summer? Both of these phenomena are due to changes in relative humidity, changes which are brought about by the heating or cooling of air in our homes with no corresponding change in absolute humidity.

First let's examine the case of dryness in winter. Remember that at low temperatures, air can hold very little water. When the cold outside air enters your house and is heated, its absolute humidity stays the same but its *relative* humidity greatly decreases. Humidifiers, which put water vapor back into the air, raise the relative humidity inside the house back to a comfortable level.

Now take the opposite case, which occurs in the summer. Recall that warm air can hold more water than cold air. When warm air from outside enters your basement, which is generally cooler than the rest of the house, the absolute humidity stays the same but the *relative* humidity increases. This results in dampness, a condition that favors the growth of mildew. To counter this effect some people use dehumidifiers, which take water out of the air.

into it. For this reason, puddles of water, as well as clothes on a line, dry more quickly when it's windy (and warm) than when it's still (or cold).

RELATIVE HUMIDITY

The absolute humidity of an **air parcel** is merely a measure of how much water vapor is in the air. But this tells us little without the proper context. A much more meaningful description of the moisture content of the air is the **relative humidity.** This tells us *how* saturated the air is. In other words, it expresses humidity as a percentage of the total moisture the air can hold. To find the relative humidity of a parcel of air, divide the amount of water vapor present in the air by the maximum amount of water the air at that temperature can hold. Then multiply by 100 to find the percentage.

As an example, consider two different parcels of air. The first air parcel has a volume of 1 cubic yard and a temperature of 50°F (10°C). It contains .4 cubic inches of water vapor. At that temperature, a cubic yard of air is capable of holding .44 cubic inches of water. Thus, the relative humidity is .4 divided by .44 times 100, which equals 91 percent. The second cubic yard of air has a temperature of about 75°F (24°C) and contains .7 cubic inches of water vapor. At that temperature, the air can hold 1.07 cubic inches of water. The relative humidity of the second parcel is 65 percent. Thus, while the second air parcel has a higher absolute humidity, the first parcel has a higher relative humidity.

You can extrapolate from the above example to understand why the relative humidity is higher at night than during the day. Consider a day in which the absolute humidity is .5 cubic inches of water per cubic yard of air. Say the temperature peaks in the afternoon at about 85°F (30°C). At that temperature, a cubic yard of air can hold 1.42 cubic inches of water. Thus the relative humidity is 35 percent. In the evening, the temperature drops to about 60°F (15°C), at which point a cubic yard of air can hold only .6 cubic inches of water. If the absolute humidity remains the same, the relative humidity rises to 83 percent.

DEW POINT

Another measure of humidity is called the **dew point.** The dew point is the temperature at which a given parcel of air becomes saturated (reaches 100 percent relative humidity) and water vapor begins to con-

Relative Humidity

This table shows the relative humidity of air with 0.6 cubic inches of water vapor per cubic yard of air at various temperatures.

Temperature of the air	Vapor air can hold	Vapor actually in the air	Relative humidity
86°F	1.42	0.60	42%
77°F	1.07	0.60	56%
68°F	0.81	0.60	74%
59°F	0.60	0.60	100%

dense, or return to the liquid phase. The dew point is so-named because it is the temperature at which dew forms on the ground.

Consider the following example in which a cubic yard of air contains .6 cubic inches of water vapor. During the day, when the temperature reaches 75°F (24°C), the air is capable of holding 1.07 cubic inches of water vapor. At that point it has a relative humidity of 56 percent. As the temperature falls (and the absolute humidity remains the same), the relative humidity increases. When the temperature reaches about 60°F (15°C), the relative humidity is 100 percent, the air is saturated, and dew begins to form. Thus, 60°F is the air's dew point. Where the absolute humidity is higher, the dew point is higher; and where absolute humidity is lower, the dew point is lower.

CONDENSATION

At the dew point, water vapor condenses to the liquid state. The form this liquid water takes depends on two factors: the distance above Earth's surface at which **condensation** occurs and the temperature of that medium. When water condenses on Earth's surface itself, it forms either **dew** or **frost.** When water condenses in the air just above the ground it forms **fog.** At higher levels, it condenses to form clouds. Here we'll look at the formation of dew, frost, and fog. In the next section we'll work through the complex process by which clouds are formed.

Morning dew drops on a flower.

Dew

You've probably experienced the feeling of wet grass on your bare feet, particularly during spring or fall. This wetness is dew, the condensation of water vapor on a cold surface. It occurs whenever the ground is cold enough to reduce the temperature of the air directly above it to the dew point. This assumes that the dew point is above freezing. If the dew point is below freezing, frost will form.

Dew forms only on surfaces that lose heat quickly and become colder than the dew point of the air, such as the surface of grass and plants. You won't find dew on the pavement or a ball diamond, because hard surfaces like these retain more heat than the air. Thus, the air above hard surfaces seldom reaches its dew point.

Dew is more likely to form on clear nights than on cloudy nights. The reason for this tendency is that Earth's surface radiates heat upward at night, while there is no incoming solar heat to warm the surface back up. Clouds trap some of that heat and re-radiate toward the ground. In the absence of clouds, that heat is lost into space. Thus, on clear nights surface temperatures drop more dramatically than they do on cloudy nights.

Dew formation plays an important role in the regulation of air temperature. The reason is that when water changes from a gas to a liquid it releases **latent heat,** the same energy it absorbed during the evaporation process. When dew forms, it warms the air around it, thus slowing the rate at which the temperature drops throughout the night. It does this so efficiently that nighttime temperatures generally don't drop below the dew point. An exception to this rule occurs when a cold air mass enters a region during the night, causing a sharp decline in temperature.

Now you can see why weather forecasts often give both the temperature and the dew point. The temperature may tell you the current condition, but the dew point tells you what to expect at night. Remember, at the dew point, **relative humidity** is close to 100 percent. On a day when temperatures are high, the dew point will also be high, say around 70°F (21°C). You can then expect night air to be in the 70s with nearly 100 percent humidity.

Frost

Frost formation is very similar to dew formation, except it occurs at temperatures below freezing. In contrast to dew, frost will form on any surface, even dirt and concrete. During winter, these surfaces become sufficiently cold for moisture to gather. Dirt and concrete don't absorb enough heat during a winter day for them to remain warmer than the **frost point** of the night air.

Central to an explanation of frost formation is a concept of **supercooled water.** Supercooled water is water that exists in a liquid form below 32°F (0°C), the freezing point of water. When the dew point is below 32°F (0°C), water vapor first condenses on a surface as "supercooled dew" and then freezes. This initial layer of frost grows as water vapor from the air freezes directly on to it.

The process of water changing directly from a gas to solid ice without first passing through the liquid phase is called **deposition.** The reverse of deposition, when ice passes directly from the solid state to water vapor without first melting, is called **sublimation.** During the process of deposition, latent heat is released to the environment. During sublimation, it is absorbed.

Frost that is formed by the process of deposition is called "true frost" or **hoar frost.** Hoar frost has the intricate structure that you can see on a windshield on a cold winter day. You may also find hoar frost formations on the inside of the windows—or between the panes of double-pane glass—in your home. Water vapor freezes onto a window when the air just inside the window is cooled to the dew point, provided the dew point is below 32°F (0°C).

Hoar frost in New Zealand.

WEATHER REPORT: SUPERCOOLED WATER

Imagine this not-so-unusual winter scene: a cold rain falls and forms icicles on houses and trees, as well as sheets of nearly impassable ice on the ground. Why is it that the water is liquid in the air, yet becomes ice when it strikes a surface? The answer lies in the mechanics of **supercooled water.**

Supercooled water is water that exists in a liquid state below 32°F (0°C). The reason why it has not frozen is that it takes more than just cold temperatures to make water freeze. It also takes a **freezing nucleus.** A freezing nucleus is a particle of ice or other solid on which water vapor can condense. In the absence of a freezing nucleus, a water droplet will not turn to ice until it cools to around -40°F (-40°C). Most freezing rain contains some ice crystals. Once those ice crystals hit the ground, they provide the freezing nuclei around which supercooled raindrops can form ice.

Another type of frost is produced by the freezing of dew that has already formed on a surface. This occurs when the dew point is above freezing and the temperature later falls below 32°F (0°C). This type of frost does not form crystal structures like hoar frost, but droplets of ice.

FOG

Fog is condensation that occurs in lower levels of air. It is essentially a cloud that has formed close to Earth's surface. Fog in temperate regions is composed of water droplets; in polar and arctic regions it may also be composed of ice crystals. Condensation in the air is generally defined as a "fog" when it restricts visibility to 1 kilometer. If visibility is greater than 1 kilometer, the condition is defined as "**mist.**" For the purposes of this discussion, we'll refer to all condensation in the lower levels of air as "fog."

The process of condensation in the air begins with **condensation nuclei.** Similar to dew and frost, which won't form in the absence of a surface, the water droplets that constitute fog and clouds need something to cling to. Condensation nuclei are tiny solid particles suspended in the air. Even in relatively clean air, there are about two thousand of these particles in every cubic inch. Examples of condensation nuclei include pollen, sea salt, sand, volcanic dust, factory smoke, and other industrial pollutants.

As has been shown in experiments using purified air, individual water vapor molecules do not readily stick together. Even when they do collide and form tiny droplets, those droplets will likely disintegrate. It has been theorized that in the absence of condensation nuclei, water would not condense into raindrops. Rather, the air would grow increasingly saturated with water vapor until it was unable to hold another molecule. Then water would fall to the ground in massive, destructive sheets.

There are several types of fog, which differ according to the conditions under which that fog was formed. Fog is produced in one of two ways: either when air is cooled to its dew point by contact with a cold surface; or when air is brought to its **saturation point** by **evaporation** from a wet surface. What follows is a brief outline of three major categories of fog. (For a more detailed discussion on this topic, see "Fog," page 109.)

The first type of fog, with which most people in the non-coastal states of the United States are familiar, is **radiation fog** (sometimes called **ground fog**). This type of fog forms on clear summer nights when winds are nearly still. After sunset, heat radiates away from the ground, cooling the ground and the air above it. Once this air is cooled to the dew point, water vapor condenses and forms a fog. When the sun rises the next morning and warms the air, the fog quickly dissipates.

The second type of fog is called **advection fog.** This is the thickest and most persistent type of fog and may form at any time of day or night. Advection fog is formed by advection, the horizontal movement of air. Specifically, it forms when a warm, moist layer of air crosses over a cold surface. The air loses heat to the cold surface. Once the air cools to the **dew point,** fog is formed.

A third class of fog is called **evaporation fog.** Like advection fog, it involves the interaction of cold air and warm air. But unlike advection fog—where warm, humid air travels over the cold air—the cold air in this case travels over a warmer body of water. Evaporation fog usually forms over inland lakes and rivers in the fall, when the air is cool but the water still retains heat. Water evaporates from the lake or river, saturates the cold air, and condenses. This fog often appears as "steam" that rises from a body of water.

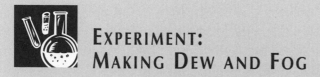

EXPERIMENT: MAKING DEW AND FOG

In this experiment you will simulate the conditions under which dew and fog are produced, namely, the interaction of warm, moist air and a cold surface. To create a cold surface, fill a metal baking pan with ice and let it stand until the pan is very cold. Next pour an inch or two of warm water into a glass jar. Then put the pan on top of the jar and observe.

You should notice two things. One is that fog forms inside the jar and the other is that dew forms on the sides of the jar. Both effects are due to the cooling effect of the ice-cold pan. The pan cools the air, causing the water vapor to condense into a fog. It also cools the sides of the jar, on which the water vapor forms dew.

CLOUD FORMATION

The subject of cloud formation has already been touched upon several times in this volume. In the section on **air pressure** we learned that as air rises, it cools. And once the air reaches the **dew point,** water vapor within it begins to condense into clouds. From our discussion of **front**s, we learned that when a **cold front** advances into a **warm front,** the warm air is thrust upward in a powerful **convection** which produces tall clouds. Finally, in the preceding section on condensation we learned that when water condenses on the ground it forms **dew** or **frost,** and when it condenses in the air it forms **fog** or clouds.

In this section we will review these concepts and explore in greater detail how and why **condensation** occurs in the upper air. We'll examine the conditions and processes responsible for creating clouds of various sizes, shapes, and compositions, at different altitudes.

WHY RISING AIR COOLS AND FALLING AIR WARMS

Both the cooling of air as it rises and the warming of air as it falls are **adiabatic** [add-ee-uh-BAT-ick] **process**es. In an adiabatic process no heat is exchanged between a moving **air parcel** and the ambient (surrounding) air, even as the temperature of the air parcel changes. When we speak of an "air parcel," we are referring to a volume of air that has a consistent temperature throughout, and experiences minimal mixing with the surrounding air. The mechanism by which ascending air cools is called **expansional cooling.** Conversely, the mechanism by which descending air warms is called **compressional warming.**

Expansional cooling is the most significant process in the formation of clouds. It works like this: as a parcel of air rises, the pressure of the air around and above it decreases. This decrease occurs because the density of air decreases with altitude. With fewer molecules, air exerts less pressure. In order to equalize its pressure with that of the ambient air, molecules within the parcel push outward, enlarging the parcel. However, the number of molecules within the parcel does not change. The result is that the same number of molecules are spread over a greater area. In other words the density of the air parcel decreases.

The expansion of air requires energy. That energy comes in the form of molecular **kinetic energy** (energy of motion), which is the same as heat. Before expanding, the molecules store that kinetic energy, meaning they are warmer. Once the molecules spend kinetic energy moving away from one another, they slow down and collide less frequently. They have a decreased kinetic energy, which is to say they have become cooler.

Conversely, as an air parcel falls, it is compressed by the increasing pressure of the surrounding air. The parcel is squeezed into a smaller volume, thereby increasing the density of the air within it. This leads to a greater number of collisions between molecules, hence greater kinetic energy. The increase in kinetic energy within the air parcel translates into an increase in temperature.

TEMPERATURE CHANGES IN UNSATURATED AIR. The change in temperature of a rising or falling air parcel is a measurable quantity. For air that is not yet at the **saturation point** (having less than 100 percent relative humidity), the rate of change is called the **dry adiabatic lapse rate.** This rate of change is constant. Air cools by about 5°F (-15°C) for every 1,000 feet (304 meters) it ascends and warms by 5°F for every 1,000 feet it descends.

TEMPERATURE CHANGES IN SATURATED AIR. Once air becomes saturated, the rate at which temperature changes with altitude occurs more slowly and is no longer a constant. The scale that applies to **saturated air** is called the **moist adiabatic lapse rate.**

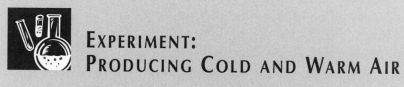

EXPERIMENT: PRODUCING COLD AND WARM AIR

This experiment demonstrates how air cools when its pressure is lowered and air warms when its pressure is raised. You will need a bicycle tire, pump, and thermometer.

First, pump up your bicycle tire until it is firm. Then take the temperature of the air in the room and record it. Now place the thermometer next to the tire valve and press down the valve to release some air. Take another reading from the thermometer and compare it to the first one. The second reading should be lower than the first because the escaping air cools as its pressure decreases.

Now it's time create warm air. Pump up the tire until it's firm again, then feel the valve. The valve is warm because the air inside the tire is being compressed and its pressure increased.

The reason that saturated air cools more slowly than unsaturated air as it rises is that water vapor condenses within saturated air (and forms a cloud), releasing **latent heat.** Whereas latent energy is absorbed in the process of **evaporation,** it is liberated in the process of condensation.

Thus as water vapor condenses out of saturated air, it releases latent heat and raises the temperature of the air parcel. This increase in temperature, however, is not enough to offset the decrease in temperature due to expansional cooling. It merely slows the rate at which the cooling occurs.

The amount by which the release of latent heat slows the cooling of an ascending air parcel depends upon that parcel's temperature. In the warmest saturated air, cooling proceeds at a rate of about 2°F (-17°C) for every 1,000 feet (304 meters) ascended. In the coldest saturated air, cooling proceeds at a rate of around 5°F (-15°C) for every 1,000 feet ascended. The average moist adiabatic lapse rate, about 3°F (-16°C) per 1,000 feet, is often used as a constant, for convenience in weather forecasting.

The reason that the moist adiabatic lapse rate depends upon temperature is that when the air parcel first becomes saturated (and is at its warmest), condensation within it releases the most latent heat. In this case, it offsets the declining temperature by the greatest amount. As the saturated air continues to rise, it cools. At the same time, the air parcel can hold a smaller amount of water vapor. The rate of condensation decreases and the release of latent heat declines. As a parcel of saturated air decreases in temperature, it provides less of a buffer to the expansional cooling.

By the same token, as saturated air descends, it warms at the moist adiabatic lapse rate. As air sinks and its temperature rises, water droplets (and clouds) evaporate into it. The process of evaporation absorbs latent heat and impedes the rate at which the temperature of the air rises. In other words, evaporation partially offsets compressional warming. Once the falling air is no longer saturated and the water droplets within it have all evaporated, it begins warming at the dry adiabatic lapse rate.

Using the dry adiabatic lapse rate, it is possible to determine the temperature of an unsaturated air parcel at various heights within the atmosphere, provided we know its temperature at the surface. And if we know the air parcel's dew point, it is possible to determine at what height clouds will form. Knowledge of air temperature at all levels of the **troposphere** is a critical element in creating **weather forecast**s.

AIR STABILITY AND VERTICAL MOTION

The vertical movement—or lack thereof—of an air parcel is dictated by differences in temperature and density between the air parcel and

Stable air: Smoke from a brush fire is trapped within a stable inversion layer at the base of the Colorado Rockies.

the ambient air. Those differences and the resultant degree of vertical movement of air are referred to as **air stability** (also called "atmospheric stability"). Air stability is the key to both the size and shape of the clouds and the intensity of the **precipitation** that results when a rising parcel of air reaches the dew point.

The rules of air stability state that as long as an air parcel has a higher temperature and lower density than the surrounding air, it will rise. When this parcel is no longer warmer than the air around it—when its pressure and density have become equal to those of its surroundings—the air parcel stops rising. On the other hand, as long as an air parcel has a lower temperature and higher density than the air around it, it will continue to fall.

A **stable air layer** marks the end point of an air parcel's vertical journey. A layer of air is stable at the height where an air parcel reaches the temperature of the ambient air and ceases to move. An **unstable air layer** is one through which an air parcel moves upward or downward. In other words, a layer of air is unstable at heights where an ascending parcel is warmer than the ambient air or a descending parcel is colder than the ambient air. If we know the surface temperature of a rising air parcel and the temperature of the troposphere at various heights, we can determine the height of a stable air layer.

In order for clouds to form, unstable conditions must exist at least long enough for a rising parcel of air to reach its dew point. And for

Unstable air: Smoke from a brush fire mixes rapidly upwards on a hot, sunny afternoon as it is blown downwind by brisk winds.

cloudy skies to turn clear—caused by a descending parcel of air—unstable conditions must also exist. In stable atmospheric conditions, where the **relative humidity** is high enough, fog may form and, prevented from rising, will persist.

WHAT CAUSES AIR STABILITY AND INSTABILITY. Unstable conditions exist within the troposphere when relatively cold air layers are situated above relatively warm surface air. This is what most commonly occurs, as air generally cools off with increasing altitude. Sometimes, however, a layer of warm air exists above colder air. This produces stable conditions. The warm air layer acts as a ceiling, or an upper limit, beyond which warm air parcels will rise no farther. There are various factors that lead the development of both stable and unstable conditions.

Air becomes stable when either an upper layer of air warms or the surface air cools. The former may be caused by a warm air mass blowing in above, while the layer of air below experiences no change in temperature. The other route to stability—the cooling of the surface air—may occur when the ground loses heat at night or a cold air mass arrives.

An absolutely stable atmosphere is produced by an **inversion.** An inversion is a condition in which air temperature increases with height. An inversion can occur when a thick layer of unsaturated air sinks, covering a large area. Since the upper levels of the air layer cover a greater vertical distance than the lower levels, the air within them has farther to fall—and more time to undergo compressional warming. The top of the layer therefore becomes warmer than the air below it. The relatively warm air layer acts a lid on any rising air parcel, preventing it from rising further. The presence of low-lying fog, **haze,** and **smog** are all indicators that an inversion has occurred near the surface.

Air instability is caused by the opposite conditions that produce stability, either the warming of the surface air or the cooling of an upper layer of air. The warming of the surface air may be caused by the absorption of solar heat by the ground during the day or the influx of a warm air mass. Or a mass of cold air might be brought in by the **winds aloft,** while the layer of air below experiences no change in temperature.

The stability of air over land changes significantly throughout the day, from the most unstable at the warmest time of day to the most stable at the coldest time of night. At night the ground loses heat and the air just above it cools. At sunrise this stability can be witnessed (in clear, calm weather) as fog rests on the ground. As the day progresses, the surface layer of air is heated by the sun. When it becomes warmer than the air above, unstable conditions prevail. As the lower air continues to warm and the difference between lower and upper layers increases, instability increases. Thus, instability is greatest at the hottest time of day. As day passes into night, the surface air cools and the cycle begins again.

AIR STABILITY AND CLOUD SHAPES. When the air is unstable, parcels of air rise throughout the day. If they rise high enough to cool to the dew point, clouds will form. In some cases, the unstable air layer is shallow, meaning that at a relatively low altitude the ambient air becomes warmer than the rising air parcel. In such cases, the clouds that form are puffy and small. If, however, the layer of unstable air is deep, tall clouds such as those that bring **thunderstorm**s may form.

When the air is stable, you won't find individual pockets of rising air, hence no puffy clouds. Clouds form in stable conditions only when an entire layer of air rises. This occurs when air flows into the center of a low-pressure area and rises or when a warm front advances and slides over a cold **air mass.** In those cases, the lifting of warm air produces a nearly continuous, flat sheet of clouds.

On a typical day, you may see both types of clouds at the same time. The reason for this pattern is that layers of stable and unstable air may be stacked on top of one another over a single location on the ground. As a result, small puffy clouds and sheets of clouds form at different altitudes.

THE LIFTING OF AIR

Air does not just rise spontaneously: it needs a push. That push comes in three different forms: convection, **frontal uplift,** and **orographic lifting.**

Convection is the lifting of air that has been heated. When heat is applied, air molecules move more quickly. The molecules spread out, the air loses density, and the air becomes thinner. As long as it is warmer and lighter than the surrounding air, it continues to rise.

Convection occurs when the ground is heated by the sun. That heat is then radiated upward from the ground, warming the air above it. This causes air parcels, often referred to as "bubbles," to rise and form individual, puffy clouds upon reaching the dew point.

Frontal uplift and orographic lifting each cause an entire mass of warm air to rise. Frontal uplift occurs when a warm air mass and a cold air mass come together at a front. The cold air mass occupies the space closest to the surface while the warm air mass rises over the cold air. As the warm air mass reaches the dew point, it forms a sheet of clouds. Orographic lifting occurs when a warm air mass encounters a mountain and rides upward along the surface. This process results in a variety of unusual cloud types, including those shaped like banners and those shaped like flying saucers. (For more information on cloud types, see "Clouds," page 75.)

CLOUDS AND PRECIPITATION

Although they cover, on average, 60 percent of the sky, clouds hold just one-one thousandth of 1 percent (0.001 percent) of the world's water. Nonetheless, they are critical elements in the cycling of water from the ground into the air and back. Without clouds to regulate the intensity of solar heat, all water would evaporate and Earth would experience an interminable **drought.** Clouds also trap heat that is re-radiated up from the ground, preventing the surface from growing too cold.

In the previous section we learned how clouds are formed. Now we will find out just what they are made of and what causes **precipitation** to form within them.

ANATOMY OF A CLOUD

A cloud is a collection of many billions of water droplets, condensed from air that has cooled to its **dew point.** Those water droplets may take one of two forms: liquid water or ice crystals. Whether they form as a liquid or as ice depends on the temperature of the air. When **condensation** occurs within air that is warmer than 32°F (0°C), it takes the form of liquid droplets. When the temperature of the air is 32°F or below, condensation usually takes the form of ice.

Clouds of liquid water droplets include another vital set of ingredients: **condensation nuclei.** A condensation nucleus is any solid particle in the air. As explained in the section on **fog,** sea salt, dust, pollen, sand, and industrial pollutants all act as nuclei around which molecules of water condense.

There are various ways in which ice crystals form within clouds, depending on atmospheric conditions. Ice crystals may either be produced by the freezing of liquid water droplets or the **deposition** of water vapor.

First, let's consider the freezing of water droplets. At temperatures below -40°F (-40°C), water freezes directly into ice, in a process called

QUESTION: WHAT KEEPS THE CLOUDS FROM FALLING?

This is a question that stumped weather watchers for centuries. It used to be a commonly held belief that the clouds were made of tiny floating bubbles. It wasn't until this century that meteorologists discovered the true reason: that cloud droplets are too small and travel too slowly to overcome the air resistance that pushes them upward.

Technically speaking, the cloud droplets lack the necessary **terminal velocity** to reach the ground. Terminal velocity, also known as the "maximum rate of fall," is the constant speed at which an object falls when the upward force of air resistance equals the downward pull of gravity. It rests on the principle that as an object nears the ground, resistance due to air pressure increases while gravity remains the same. An object can never fall at a rate faster than its terminal velocity.

spontaneous nucleation. However, at higher temperatures the process becomes more complicated. Except for the largest droplets, water will not assume the crystalline structure of ice in the absence of **freezing nuclei.** Freezing nuclei are solid particles, such as clay, vegetable debris, or ice crystals themselves, suspended in the air, upon which water droplets freeze. Freezing nuclei serve a function in the formation of ice crystals similar to that of condensation nuclei in the formation of water droplets.

Freezing nuclei exist in the atmosphere in relatively small numbers and are sometimes in short supply within clouds where temperatures are below 32°F (0°C). This accounts for the presence of **supercooled water,** water that exists in a liquid state below the freezing point, within some clouds (see box, page 53.)

The second method of forming ice crystals, the deposition of water vapor, happens much less frequently than does the freezing of water droplets. Deposition only occurs at temperatures below -4°F (-20°C) and in the presence of special freezing nuclei called **deposition nuclei.** Deposition nuclei, examples of which include ash, diatoms, and spores, are relatively rare in the atmosphere.

Since air temperature generally declines with increasing altitude, we most often find ice-crystal clouds at the highest levels of the **troposphere**; liquid-water clouds at lower levels; and clouds containing both liquid and ice at middle levels.

WHAT MAKES RAIN AND SNOW FALL

In order for water to fall to the ground as rain, water droplets in clouds have to become large enough—and obtain a terminal velocity great enough—to reach the ground. It takes from one million to fifteen million water droplets to form an average raindrop, which is about .08 inches (2 millimeters) in diameter. Whereas the terminal velocity of a water droplet is about .02 mph (.03 kph), the terminal velocity of a raindrop is about 15 mph (24 kph).

Just how do cloud droplets grow to the size of a raindrop? The most obvious answer is condensation. That is, more and more water vapor molecules condense to a liquid until drops of water become large enough to fall to the ground. This process alone, however, is quite slow and cannot possibly account for amount and rate of rainfall we experience in the **middle latitudes.** Rain often starts falling just thirty minutes after a cloud begins forming. Condensation alone can not produce drops of water large enough to fall, during that time.

Early in this century, scientists discovered the answer: ice. Ice crystals often exist together with supercooled water droplets in clouds. Such clouds are called **cold clouds.**

Ice crystals grow more quickly than, and at the expense of, water droplets in cold clouds. The reason for this has to do with **vapor pressure,** the pressure exerted by a vapor when it is in equilibrium with its liquid or solid. Equilibrium is defined as the **saturation point,** the point at which the same number of molecules are entering and leaving the gaseous state.

Within cold clouds, vapor pressure is greater over the surface of a water droplet than it is over the surface of an ice crystal. This pressure differential creates a force which directs water vapor molecules away from the water droplets and toward the ice crystals. In the process, it lowers the pressure over the water droplets. To maintain equilibrium, more molecules then evaporate from the surface of water droplets which, in turn, are directed toward the ice crystals. Each time the cycle repeats, the ice crystals grow larger and the water droplets grow smaller.

When an ice crystal becomes large enough, it begins to fall, attract-

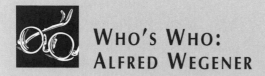

WHO'S WHO: ALFRED WEGENER

Alfred Wegener (1880–1930) was the German meteorologist and geophysicist who solved the mystery of raindrops. He reasoned that **supercooled** raindrops often coexist with ice crystals in clouds. And ice crystals, which have a lower vapor pressure than liquid water, attract water molecules to them.

Although this discovery was remarkable, Wegener is more famous for developing the theory of **continental drift** in 1912. This theory states that 200 to 250 million years ago all land on Earth was joined together in one huge continent. Over the years forces deep within the earth caused the land to break apart and the chunks to move away from one another, eventually reaching their current configuration.

After first pursuing astronomy, in the early 1900s Wegener switched to geology and meteorology. At the time, the study of weather was a new scientific discipline. Wegener and his brother conducted numerous experiments with weather balloons and kites. During an international contest in 1906 they flew aboard a balloon for fifty-two consecutive hours, setting a world record.

Wegener also made four trips to Greenland to study glaciers and **climate.** It was during his final trip to that frigid land, on his fiftieth birthday, that Wegener died of heart failure.

For further reading on Alfred Wegener, see Witze, Alexandra. "Alfred Wegener." *Notable Twentieth-Century Scientists.* Vol. 4. Ed. Emily J. McMurray. Detroit: Gale Research Inc., 1995.

ing water molecules as it goes. Usually, during its descent, it takes on the form of a **snowflake.**

If the air warms above the freezing point during an ice crystal's descent, the ice melts and hits the ground as rain. If the air remains below freezing, we'll get snow.

Ice crystals within clouds, however, can't account for all precipitation. In the tropics there are **warm clouds,** clouds that are too warm to contain ice. Yet these clouds still produce plenty of rain. This leads to the conclusion that in warm clouds, water droplets must collide to form bigger drops. While meteorologists are still seeking to answer the question of just how this happens, one current theory is that large droplets form around giant sea-salt condensation nuclei and that these large droplets become even larger by colliding with smaller droplets.

THE WATER CYCLE

Precipitation represents one portion of the **water cycle** (or "hydrologic cycle"), the continuous exchange of water between the atmosphere and the oceans and landmasses on Earth's surface. The other side of this equation is **evaporation,** the process by which liquid water at Earth's surface is converted to a gas and is returned to the atmosphere. Some of that water vapor then forms clouds which return the water to Earth as rain or snow.

Now we'll examine the water cycle in more detail. Most of Earth's water—about 97.2 percent—exists in the oceans. The rest, save the .001 of 1 percent that exists as water vapor in the atmosphere, is contained in the polar ice caps. All three phases of water—solid, liquid and gas—continually co-exist on Earth. The water cycle is driven by the continuous conversion of water molecules among these three phases.

Eighty-five to 90 percent of the moisture that enters the atmosphere comes from the oceans. The rest evaporates from the soil, vegetation, lakes, and rivers that exist on the continental landmasses. Even plants emit water through tiny pores in the underside of their leaves in a process called **transpiration.**

Some of the moist air above oceans is carried overland by the wind. Clouds form and swell and drop rain and snow on the ground. When precipitation hits the ground, it either sinks into the surface or runs off, depending on the surface composition. For example, rainwater will sink into soil and sand. The excess water will form puddles on the surface or seep down into underground streams or reservoirs. Water found under Earth's surface is known as groundwater. If the water strikes a hard surface, like rock or pavement, it will either run off and flow into rivers and lakes or drip through cracks and make its way to the groundwater.

The oceans experience a net loss of water in this portion of the cycle. More water evaporates from them than returns as precipitation.

This deficit is corrected when water in rivers and streams flows back into the oceans. Thus the **global water budget**—the volume of water coming and going from the oceans, atmosphere, and continental landmasses—is kept in balance.

LAND AND WEATHER

The different properties of land and sea result in the formation of different weather patterns over each. The two major differences between land and sea can be loosely categorized as heat retention and surface features. These characteristics affect temperature highs and lows, cloud formation, and storm systems. And, as we'll see, certain types of **topography** (physical features of land) create their own small-scale weather patterns.

HEAT RETENTION

Land heats up and cools down relatively quickly, whereas water is slower to absorb heat and slower to release it. Water absorbs and stores heat in a form called **latent heat.** Latent heat does not affect the temperature of water, but is the energy used to drive changes in phase from solid to liquid or liquid to gas.

The fact that land rapidly absorbs solar heat during the day, and rapidly loses heat at night, results in greater temperature extremes on land than one finds at sea. You may have experienced these differences in heat retention if you've ever gone swimming both in the afternoon and in the evening on a summer day. When you swim in the heat of the day, the water feels cooler than the air. Yet once the sun goes down and the air temperature drops, the water becomes the warmer medium.

SEA AND LAND BREEZES. Two manifestations of the temperature differential (and corresponding **pressure gradient**) created between land and water throughout the day are **sea breeze**s and **land breeze**s. These are the breezes that you feel at the beach. The sea breeze blows toward shore during the day, when the sand is warmer than the water, and the land breeze blows toward the water during the night, when the water is warmer than the sand.

During the day, when the sand warms quickly, a low-pressure area is created over the sand. In comparison, a high-pressure area forms over the water. A gentle wind flows from the high-pressure to the low-pressure (from the water to the sand). This is known as a sea breeze.

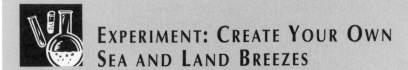

EXPERIMENT: CREATE YOUR OWN SEA AND LAND BREEZES

Take two baking pans and fill one with sand and the other with ice. Warm the sand gently in the oven on low heat. Place the two pans side by side. Now create a wind screen out of a long piece of cardboard, bent into three sections. Stand it upright so it fits along the back and two sides of your side-by-side pans.

Now light an incense stick or cone and hold it at the boundary between the two pans. Observe which way the smoke (your simulated "sea breeze") blows. To create a "land breeze," replace the ice with warm water in one pan, allow the sand to cool in the other, and repeat the experiment.

At night, the sand loses heat more quickly than does the water, so the process is reversed. The breeze flows from the high-pressure area over the sand, out to the low-pressure area over the water. This is known as a land breeze.

MOUNTAIN WEATHER

The peaks and valleys of a mountain range alter the behavior of a large-scale weather system as it travels across the mountains. These surface features also produce small-scale weather patterns unique to that topography. For instance, as we saw in the section on storms, a storm slows as it crosses a mountain range and re-intensifies on the other side. The reason is that when a storm travels over a mountain, the storm center becomes flattened between the mountaintop and the top of the **troposphere.** The spinning winds at the storm center are therefore forced to expand horizontally, which slows the spinning. When the storm emerges on the other side of the mountain, it has more room to stretch out vertically and spins faster again.

Mountains also produce distinct, small-scale weather patterns that are limited to the mountainous area. For instance, some clouds have unique shapes that resemble banners or disks. These clouds form at the tops of mountains and are the products of **orographic lifting.** Orographic lifting is the process in which a warm air mass rides upward along the surface of a mountain. As the air rises it cools. Once it reaches the **dew point, condensation** occurs and clouds form.

The rain that comes from these clouds generally falls on the peak and the westward, or **windward,** side of the mountain, the side on which the warm air ascended. On the other side of the mountain—the eastward or **leeward** side—conditions are much drier. The reason is that as air descends across the leeward side it warms, causing water droplets and clouds to evaporate. The uneven distribution of **precipitation** across a mountain is known as the **rain-shadow effect.**

A rain-shadow may occupy the base of a single large mountain or the entire region east of a mountain range. An example of the former is Mount Waialeale on the island of Kauai in Hawaii. The windward side of this mountain is considered the rainiest place on Earth. Near the peak of the mountain, the windward side receives on average 40 feet (12 meters) of rainfall a year. The leeward side of the mountain, in contrast, is extremely dry. It receives only 20 inches (50 centimeters) of rainfall, on average, each year.

A larger-scale rain-shadow effect occurs east of the Rocky Mountains, in the high plains of the central United States. This region receives relatively little rainfall especially compared to the windward side of the Rockies. In South America, a similar situation exists in the arid region

Mountain weather: A cape of clouds forms as warm, moist air rises up the windward slope of a Hawaiian island. The air flow is from left to right. The clouds begin dissipating as they slide down the leeward side.

east of the Andes Mountains. Many of the world's deserts lie in the rain shadow of mountain ranges.

OCEANS AND WEATHER

The oceans cover more than 70 percent of our planet's surface. They have a tremendously important role in global heat distribution. What is more, they are involved (in conjunction with the winds) in generating global weather patterns and influencing **climate.** As we discussed in the section on global wind patterns the sun heats Earth unevenly and the atmosphere strives to even out heat distribution. While winds are responsible for about two-thirds of the world's heat distribution, **ocean currents** are responsible for the remaining one-third.

Oceans retain heat over long periods of time, even as the amount of energy they receive from the sun varies. While this enables ocean currents to carry heat from the equator to the poles, it also means that the temperature of the oceans is often different from that of land at similar **latitude**s. On the coasts, the exchange of cold air and warm air can generate wind, rain, and storms.

There are also seasonal differences between land and sea. While the temperature changes that accompany a new season take effect immediately on land, they lag behind by several weeks in the oceans. It isn't until several weeks after the first day of winter that oceans reach their lowest temperature of the year, and until several weeks after the first day of summer that they reach their highest temperature of the year. As a result, still-warm ocean air warms up some coastal regions as winter sets in. And still-cold ocean air slows the warming of some coastal areas in the spring.

OCEAN CURRENTS

Ocean currents are permanent or semipermanent large-scale circulations of water, at or below the ocean surface. Ocean currents are closely tied to the global circulation of winds. As the wind blows, it causes the surface layer of water to move with it. As the surface water flows, it gradually piles up and creates differences in pressure in the levels of water beneath it. The result is that deeper water moves as well. Due to the relatively high friction that exists between layers of water, ocean currents move much more slowly than the wind.

Ocean currents, like air currents, are influenced by the **Coriolis effect,** the rotational force of Earth. The Coriolis effect deflects the motion of both ocean currents and air currents to the right in the **Northern Hemi-**

sphere and to the left in the **Southern Hemisphere.** This causes surface waters to blow in a direction, on average, 45 degrees different than that of the wind. That's because once the wind starts the surface waters in motion, the direction of water flow is turned by the Coriolis effect.

Similar to the winds, ocean currents travel in a circular fashion around major high-pressure systems in the atmosphere above them. The large circular patterns of ocean currents are called **gyres** (JEE-urs). And ocean currents—like winds—travel clockwise around atmospheric high-pressure systems in the Northern Hemisphere and counterclockwise around atmospheric high-pressure areas in the Southern Hemisphere.

UPWELLING

As you can see in Figure 10, water travels in a series of loops from the equator to the poles and back. The net effect of ocean currents is to cycle heat from the warm equatorial region to the poles. While one would expect surface water to become consistently colder as it travels

Figure 10: Major ocean currents of the world.

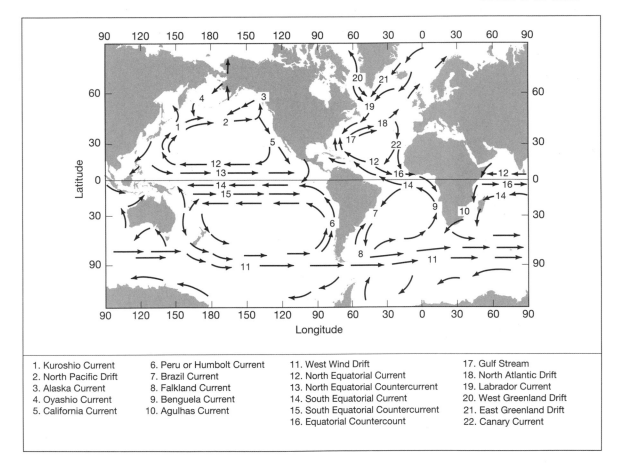

1. Kuroshio Current	6. Peru or Humbolt Current	11. West Wind Drift	17. Gulf Stream
2. North Pacific Drift	7. Brazil Current	12. North Equatorial Current	18. North Atlantic Drift
3. Alaska Current	8. Falkland Current	13. North Equatorial Countercurrent	19. Labrador Current
4. Oyashio Current	9. Benguela Current	14. South Equatorial Current	20. West Greenland Drift
5. California Current	10. Agulhas Current	15. South Equatorial Countercurrent	21. East Greenland Drift
		16. Equatorial Countercount	22. Canary Current

north and warmer as it travels south (in the Northern Hemisphere), this is not always the case. Sometimes this trend is interrupted, due to a phenomena called **upwelling.**

Upwelling is the rising of cold waters from the depths of the ocean. Upwelling occurs when surface water along a coast flows out to sea and deep water flows in and rises to replace it. This directional flow of water is set in motion when the wind blows parallel to the coastline. An example of where this occurs is Cape Mendocino, in northern California. Due to upwelling, the waters off the coast of Cape Mendocino are cooler in the summer than are the waters off the coast of Washington State, which is farther north.

Here we will give a step-by-step description of the process that is responsible for Cape Mendocino's cold waters. It begins with the winds in that region, which blow from north to south along the California coast, in a clockwise fashion around the Pacific High. The surface water is pushed southward by the wind and curved to the right by the Coriolis effect. The result is that where the wind blows parallel to the coast at Cape Mendocino, the surface water flows out to sea.

Why then does deeper water flow inward toward the coast and upward to replace the surface water? Because at great enough depths of the water, something very curious happens: the water flows in a direction that's opposite that of the surface water! That is to say, where the surface water flows out to sea, the water 100 yards (110 meters) or so below flows in toward the surface.

This changing pattern of water flow along a vertical gradient is called the **Ekman Spiral.** It works like this: First, imagine ocean water as being made up of a series of vertical layers. Each layer exerts a frictional drag on the layer beneath it, meaning that water travels more slowly the deeper you go. In addition, the Coriolis effect rotates each successively deeper layer of water further to the right than the layer above it. Thus, at great enough depths, the water flow reverses direction. In the case of Cape Mendocino, as the surface water flows out to sea, deep, cold water flows toward land. It continues upward, along the ocean floor until it meets the coast.

EL NIÑO/SOUTHERN OSCILLATION

The most striking example of how ocean currents can influence global weather patterns is a phenomena known as the **El Niño/Southern Oscillation** (ENSO). This phenomena begins as the annual warming of the waters off the coast of Peru. In years when this phenomena is stronger and more persistent than usual, it can bring drought, storms, and floods to farflung locations around the globe.

El Niño and the **Southern Oscillation** are actually two different, but interrelated and simultaneous events. Although they are usually considered in tandem, we'll discuss them individually here for the purpose of understanding what they are. El Niño, Spanish for "child," was given its name by the residents of the Peruvian coastal area. The name refers to the Christ child, since El Niño usually occurs around Christmas.

The waters off the coast of Peru are typically quite cold and nutrient-rich, the ideal habitat for fish. The area is known particularly for its anchovy populations. Once a year, however, warm waters move in from the equatorial region. These waters are nutrient-poor and unable to sustain fish. Most years, this warming persists for only a month or so before the cold waters return. Occasionally—usually once every three to seven years—the warm waters do not leave. When they remain for a year or two, the period is called a **major El Niño event.**

The most immediate consequence of a major El Niño event is felt by the coastal Peruvians, whose fishing-based economy is disrupted. And since the warm water is inhospitable to marine life, dead fish, gulls, and marine plants litter the beaches. Their decomposing carcasses and resultant increase of bacteria in the water produce a foul odor. A major El Niño event even affects the poultry industry in the United States, since

Figure 11:
El Niño and the
Southern Oscillation.

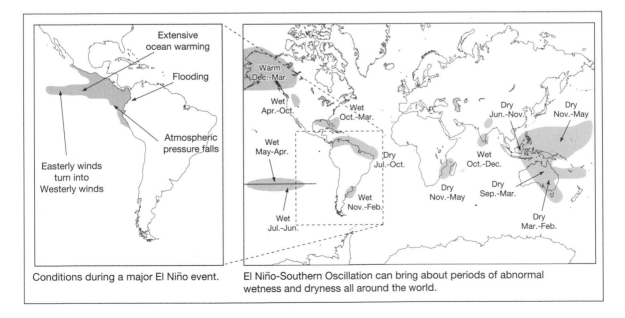

Conditions during a major El Niño event. | El Niño-Southern Oscillation can bring about periods of abnormal wetness and dryness all around the world.

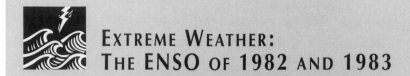

EXTREME WEATHER: THE ENSO OF 1982 AND 1983

The El Niño/Southern Oscillation of 1982 and 1983 brought about devastating **drought**s, **flood**s, and storms in farflung places across the globe. Australia was hit with its worst drought ever. Hawaii, Mexico, southern Africa, the Philippines, and Indonesia also experienced droughts. Meanwhile, extensive flooding plagued Louisiana, Florida, Cuba, Ecuador, Peru, and Bolivia. A string of violent storms traveled across the west coast of the U.S. and a series of five **hurricane**s pounded the islands of French Polynesia.

fishmeal produced in Peru is fed to chickens here. It was not until the 1950s, however, that meteorologists began to learn the larger impact of a major El Niño event and its connection with the Southern Oscillation.

The Southern Oscillation is the name given to the shifting pattern of **air pressure** that occurs between opposite ends of the Pacific Ocean in the Southern Hemisphere. Generally, pressure is higher over the eastern Pacific, near South America, and lower over the western Pacific, near Australia. This **pressure gradient** drives the **trade winds** westward, and toward the equator. Every few years, however, this pressure differential reverses. Since surface water circulations and sea level are also driven by trade winds, the Southern Oscillation has long-range effects. Weather patterns are disrupted not only throughout the Pacific region of the Southern Hemisphere, but into the Northern Hemisphere as far north as Alaska and northern Canada.

That major El Niño events and the Southern Oscillation occur in the same years (these are commonly referred to as "ENSO years") is no coincidence. It turns out that the warming of the waters off the coast of Peru results in a decrease of air pressure in the eastern Pacific. As a result, the air pressure in the western Pacific rises.

At present, ENSO is being widely studied by meteorologists. Even as it becomes easier to predict when El Niño years will occur, it remains difficult to predict how they will influence the weather at different locations. Unlocking the mystery of ENSO will surely be of great value in making long-range **weather forecast**s and predictions of climatic change.

CLOUDS

As we learned in the chapter "What Is Weather?" clouds are formed when rising air cools to its **dew point** and water droplets condense (see page 55). There are many different conditions under which this occurs, producing a variety of cloud types. The force with which the air rises, the **topography** of the surface, and the temperature at the surface and at various altitudes, are among the factors that influence whether a cloud will be small or large, thick or thin, flat or bumpy, and whether or not it will produce **precipitation.**

CLOUD CLASSIFICATION SYSTEMS

The first scientific method of classifying clouds was devised in 1803 by English naturalist and pharmacist Luke Howard (1772–1864). In an article entitled "On the Modifications of Clouds," Howard assigned Latin names to four different cloud categories, based on appearance: **cumuliform** ("piled") for puffy, heaped-up clouds; **cirriform** ("hair-like") for thin, wispy, feathery swirls of clouds; **stratiform** ("layered") for continuous, flat sheets or layers of clouds; and **nimbus** ("cloud") for dark rain clouds. He then used combinations of these names to describe other clouds. For instance **nimbostratus** is a rain-producing, layered cloud and **stratocumulus** is a continuous sheet of cloud punctuated by bumps.

This system of cloud classification was revised in 1874, at the first meeting of the International Meteorological Congress. There it was decided to use Howard's cloud names as a starting point for a classification system that placed clouds into ten categories, based on their height in the sky as well as their appearance. In 1896, the Congress published the *International Cloud Atlas,* the general outline for the system still in use today.

Low clouds are those with a base below 6,500 feet (2 kilometers); middle clouds are those with a base between 6,500 and 23,000 feet (2 and 7 kilometers); and high clouds are those with a base between 16,000 and 43,000 feet (5 kilometers and 13 kilometers). It's important to remember that, for classification purposes, it is the bottom, or base, of a cloud that determines it's height.

You may notice that there is some overlap between the altitude of cloud bases in the middle- and high-cloud categories. The altitude at which clouds form depends on air temperature. On warm days and in warmer locations, medium and high clouds form at higher altitudes than they do on cold days.

This list of cloud-base altitudes pertains only to the **middle latitudes,** or temperate regions. In the tropics, the bases of middle and high clouds form at higher altitudes than they do in temperate regions. And in the polar regions these cloud bases form at the lower altitudes than they

Figure 12:
The base heights of the
ten genera of clouds.

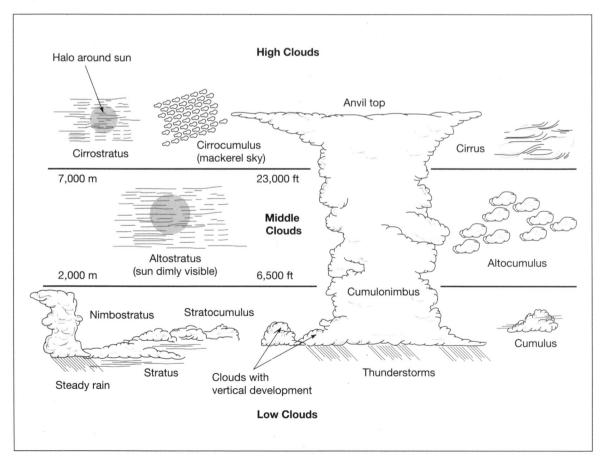

EXPERIMENT: MAKE A CLOUD IN A BOTTLE

For this experiment you will need a large glass jar (like a pickle or mayonnaise jar), a metal baking tray with ice cubes, a piece of black paper, and matches.

First, affix the black paper to the back side of the jar, so your cloud will be easier to see. Next, fill the jar about one-quarter of the way full with hot water (but not boiling water, because this can crack the glass). Then carefully light a match, hold it over the jar opening for a few seconds, and drop it into the jar. Quickly place the tray of ice on top of the jar and observe what happens inside the jar.

This experiment reproduces the circumstances under which clouds are formed. Namely, the surface is warmed, the lowest layer of air rises, and **condensation** occurs as the air cools. The smoke from the match provides the **condensation nuclei** around which water droplets form.

do in temperate regions. We will cover these concepts in greater detail later in this chapter.

There also exists a fourth group of clouds, the tops of which may extend to the edge of the **troposphere,** called towering cumuliform clouds. Sometimes towering cumuliform clouds are placed with other clouds in the "low" category, since their bases form below 10,000 feet (3 kilometers). In most classification schemes, however, including the one

Four Major Cloud Groups and Their Types			
High Clouds	**Middle Clouds**	**Low Clouds**	**Clouds with vertical development**
Cirrus (Cs)	Altostratus (As)	Stratus (St)	Cumulus (Cu)
Cirrostratus (Cs)	Altocumulus (Ac)	Stratocumulus (Sc)	Cumulonimbus (Cb)
Cirrocumulus (Cc)		Nimbostratus (Ns)	

in this book, cumuliform clouds are placed in a category of their own, called "vertical clouds."

The ten basic categories of clouds, arranged by base height and appearance, are called genera. Each genus (singular form of "genera") is subdivided into species. We will cover cloud species in greater detail later in this chapter.

LOW CLOUDS

Low clouds are almost always composed of liquid water droplets. When the temperature drops below 23°F (-5°C), however, these clouds may also contain ice crystals. There are three genera of low-lying clouds: **stratocumulus, stratus,** and **nimbostratus.**

STRATOCUMULUS (SC) [STRAY-TOE-CUE-MYE-LUSS]

Stratocumulus is one of the most common types of cloud in the world. As its name suggests, stratocumulus is a layered-puffy hybrid of a cloud. The puffiness is a result of warm air rising above the base of the cloud and condensing at higher altitudes. Stratocumulus ranges in color from white to dark gray, depending on its thickness.

Stratocumulus forms wide, shallow layers and may blanket the entire sky or may have breaks through which blue patches are visible. It

A layer of stratocumulus clouds over Seattle, Washington.

may appear as a series of distinct, yet touching, rounded masses. Sometimes those masses appear in rows.

The presence of stratocumulus is an indicator of high levels of moisture in the lower levels of the **troposphere.** It is formed either when pockets of warm air rise to the **dew point** or when a warm **air mass** is pushed upward by an advancing **front.** Usually, stratocumulus clouds do not produce **precipitation.** However, when these clouds become thick enough, they may bring **drizzle** or light snow.

Stratus (St) [STRAY-tuss]

The second type of low cloud, stratus, is that gloomy, gray, featureless sheet of cloud that covers the entire sky. It is common worldwide and is noted for blanketing coastal and mountainous areas for long periods of time. Stratus may produce drizzle or, if it's cold enough, light snow.

Stratus formation takes place at a lower altitude than any other cloud type. Stratus is most often a shallow layer of cloud, sometimes appearing nearly transparent. It may develop to a maximum thickness of 1,500 feet (450 meters). A stratus sheet typically covers an area of hundreds of square miles across.

Stratus clouds are usually formed by the rising of a large mass of moist air. In some cases, however, stratus is formed by a layer of **fog** that is warmed by the sun and rises from the ground. Alternately, the rising

Stratus clouds swirl through downtown Chicago, Illinois, some actually forming as the moist Lake Michigan air rises up and over the taller buildings.

fog may create a layer of stratus that is uneven and puffy, more accurately described as stratocumulus.

NIMBOSTRATUS (NS) [NIM-BO-**STRAY**-TUSS]

Finally, there are wet-looking nimbostratus clouds. These clouds are similar to stratus clouds in that they form a gray layer that covers all or a large part of the sky. Nimbostratus, however, are thicker and darker than stratus. They are often jagged at the base, a result of being blown about by the wind. Nimbostratus clouds may fuse with stratocumulus clouds below or **altostratus** clouds above, making their upper and lower edges difficult to distinguish.

When a layer of nimbostratus covers the sky, it is impossible to see the sun or the moon. Nimbostratus often brings continuous, light-to-heavy precipitation that lasts more than twelve hours. This precipitation may evaporate and produce a low-lying cloud or fog, further reducing visibility on the ground. The base of a nimbostratus cloud may form as high as 13,000 feet (4 kilometers) above ground. For this reason, nimbostratus is sometimes classified as part of the middle group of clouds.

MIDDLE CLOUDS

Middle clouds are those with bases that form about 6,500 feet (2 kilometers) to 23,000 feet (7 kilometers) above Earth's surface. The tem-

The sun shines dimly through altostratus clouds, as though through frosted glass.

perature of the air at this elevation is usually between 32°F (0°C) and -13°F (-25°C). Thus, these clouds contain **supercooled water** or a combination of supercooled water and ice. There are two genera of middle clouds: **altocumulus** and **altostratus.**

ALTOSTRATUS (As) [ALL-TOE-**STRAY**-TUSS]

A description of altostratus can be discerned from its name. The Latin prefix *alto-* means "high" and *stratus* means "sheet-like." Thus, altostratus clouds are flat sheets, the base of which is higher than ordinary stratus clouds. Similar to **stratus,** this plain layer of cloud covers the entire sky.

Altostratus is a white, gray, or blue-gray uniform cloud sheet that may, like stratus, blanket an area as large as hundreds of square miles. It is generally thin enough that a dim outline of the sun (called a "watery sun") or moon can be seen through it. Sometimes, however, is thick enough to entirely block our view of the sun or moon.

Altostratus can be distinguished from **nimbostratus** because nimbostratus is a darker gray and is so thick that it always hides the sun. Also, nimbostratus looks textured whereas altostratus is more likely to look smooth. And altostratus can be told from stratus because stratus is the lower and darker of the two.

Altostratus clouds are produced when a large **air mass** rises, often pushed upward by an incoming **front,** and cools to the **dew point.** When

An undercast layer of altocumulus clouds, through which a dense pall of smoke has penetrated from a forest fire raging below (seen beneath the wing of the plane).

a layer of altostratus is relatively thin, it does not generally yield **precipitation.** However, when it is thick enough it will produce rain and snow over an extensive area. Altostratus clouds often precede an advancing storm system.

ALTOCUMULUS (AC) [ALL-TOE-CUE-MYU-LUSS]

A description of **altocumulus** can also be discerned from its name, *alto-* plus *cumulus*. Altocumulus clouds are puffy masses, the bases of which are higher than **stratocumulus** clouds. Altocumulus clouds often appear in parallel rows or waves, comprised of thousands of small clouds, and may be several layers thick. These clouds are noted for the picturesque patterns they form. They are produced by the lifting of warm air that often precedes an advancing **cold front.**

Within a single altocumulus cloud, one will find areas of light and dark gray and even white. The edges of each puffy mass are pronounced, indicating the presence of water droplets.

Altocumulus clouds may be confused with **stratocumulus** clouds below. The way to tell them apart is to make a fist and stretch it toward the sky. Individual altocumulus clouds will appear to be the size of your thumbnail while individual stratocumulus clouds will appear to be the size of your fist.

A mixture of stratocumulus and altocumulus cloud fragments.

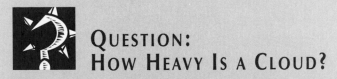

QUESTION: HOW HEAVY IS A CLOUD?

The process of determining a cloud's weight would be simple if we could coax a cloud onto a scale. Given this impossibility, we must employ a more complicated method.

The first step is to determine the volume of the cloud, that is to determine the number of cubic feet (or cubic meters) that it occupies. We'll use metric units in this example, since that is the system used by meteorologists in this task. It is simplest to measure small to medium-sized cumulus clouds, since these clouds tend to have similar values for length, width, and height.

We begin by measuring the cloud's shadow on the ground. Say that the shadow is a kilometer long. That equals 1,000 meters. We can then estimate that the cloud's width and height each measure 1,000 meters. To find the cloud's volume, multiply width by length by height, which is 1,000 x 1,000 x 1,000. This equals 1 billion cubic meters.

Then multiply the volume by the weight of water within 1 cubic meter of cumulus cloud, which has been calculated to be .5 gram. One billion cubic meters times .5 gram per cubic meter equals 500 million grams. Thus, our cloud weighs about 500,000 kilograms.

Altocumulus clouds are produced in a similar fashion to **altostratus** clouds, namely by the uplift of a large air mass and the resulting **condensation** of water droplets. The difference between the two processes has to do with **air stability:** When the atmosphere is **unstable** around the dew point, warm air continues to rise and condense. This leads to the formation of altocumulus. When the air is **stable,** altostratus is formed.

When warm air rises far above the base of altocumulus clouds, the puffy masses appear tall and are described as "little castles." When little castles are present in the morning on a warm, humid day, it is a sign that afternoon thunderstorms are likely.

HIGH CLOUDS

High clouds are those with bases situated more than 20,000 feet (6 kilometers) above Earth's surface. They are formed when water condenses out of the air at high altitudes. In very cold weather in the **middle latitudes** they may form at altitudes as low as 16,000 feet (5 kilometers). The temperature of the air where high clouds form is generally below -13°F (-25°C) and the moisture content is low. Thus, these clouds are composed mostly of ice crystals, with small amounts of liquid water. This gives them their thin, wispy appearance.

Most of the time these clouds appear white. The exceptions are at sunrise and sunset, when the sunlight is scattered in a way that makes them appear orange, red, or yellow. There are three genera of high clouds: **cirrus, cirrostratus,** and **cirrocumulus.**

CIRRUS (CI) [SIR-us]

The most common **cirriform** clouds are cirrus. These clouds are created by wind-blown ice crystals and are so thin as to be nearly transparent. Cirrus clouds may resemble long streamers, feathery patches, strands of hair with a curl at the end, or a number of other distinctive shapes. The wispy appearance of some cirrus clouds have earned them the nickname "mares' tails."

Cirrus clouds may appear in small patches or extensive areas of the

Feathery trails of ice crystals fall beneath patches of cirrus clouds.

sky. In the former case, they are associated with fair weather. These clouds are carried across the sky from west to east by the **prevailing winds.** Sailors used to measure the speed of **winds aloft** by the appearance of cirrus clouds: the longer the streamers, the faster the wind.

When the cirrus cover grows thicker in the west and takes on a criss-cross pattern, it means that warm air is advancing at high altitudes. This is the first sign of an approaching **warm front.** After that, one can expect to see the development of a thick layer of cirrostratus. Clouds will develop at progressively lower heights as the rain approaches.

CIRROSTRATUS (CS) [SIR-OH-STRAY-TUSS]

Cirrostratus clouds are a higher, thinner version of **altostratus** clouds. They cover all or part of the sky, but in a sheet thin enough that the sun or moon are clearly visible through them. When these clouds are present there is often a **halo,** a ring of light, around the sun or moon. The halo is produced by the **refraction** (bending) of light through the ice crystals within the clouds. In some cases, when cirrostratus clouds are nearly transparent, a halo is all that defines their presence. When these clouds are thicker, they appear as a milky white sheet across the sky.

Cirrostratus clouds are formed by a large-scale, gentle lifting of moist air to great heights. This rising air is a result of **convergence,** the flow of winds in toward an area on the surface.

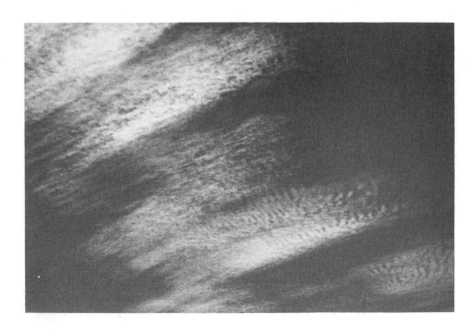

Cirrocumulus clouds.

Cirrostratus can be told from altostratus because cirrostratus is thinner and lighter in color than altostratus. Another way to tell the two cloud types apart is that only cirrostratus allows enough sunlight to pass through, to create shadows on the ground.

Snow rarely falls from cirrostratus clouds and when it does, it usually takes the form of **virga,** meaning it evaporates before it hits the ground. A layer of cirrostratus clouds that's growing thicker often represents the leading edge of a warm front. And if a band of middle clouds shows up next, you can expect rain or snow in the next twelve to twenty-four hours.

CIRROCUMULUS (CC) [SIR-OH-CUE-MYU-LUSS]

The most uncommon type of cirriform clouds are cirrocumulus. These are small, white, rounded, and puffy clouds. They may occur individually or in patterns resembling rippled waves or the scales of a fish (the latter is termed "mackerel sky"). Cirrocumulus is noted for its distinctive patterns and for the beautiful shades of red and yellow it takes on during sunrises and sunsets.

Cirrocumulus clouds resemble **altocumulus** clouds but exist at higher altitudes. The two cloud types can be told apart because cirrocumulus clouds are even-colored, as opposed to altocumulus clouds, in

Towering cumulus clouds.

which some areas are darker than others. Also, cirrocumulus clouds have smaller individual puffs than do altocumulus clouds.

Cirrocumulus clouds usually cover a small portion of the sky; only rarely do they cover the entire sky. They generally form thin layers and block very little sunlight. In fact, similar to the case of cirrostratus clouds, enough sunlight shines through cirrocumulus cloud for shadows to appear on the ground.

Cirrocumulus itself does not yield **precipitation.** However, if the cloud layer begins to thicken it may indicate that a **front** is on the way.

VERTICAL CLOUDS

The clouds included in this category are the products of sudden, forceful uplifts of small pockets of warm air. To produce a vertical cloud, the air must be thrust upward, either by **convection** or by **frontal uplift,** at a speed of about 70 miles per hour (mph) or 113 kilometers per hour (kph). In contrast, the uplift of air that produces other cloud types usually occurs at a rate of less than 1 mph (1.6 kph).

The base of a vertical cloud is usually between 3,600 and 6,600 feet (1 and 2 kilometers) above the ground. These clouds are found in all parts of the world except Antarctica, where surface temperatures are so cold that convection can not take place.

Cirrus clouds above and cumulus clouds below.

Within this category are **cumuliform** clouds, including **cumulus** and **cumulonimbus** (thunderstorm clouds). It's important to note, however, that **altostratus** and **nimbostratus** demonstrate varying degrees of vertical development, and for that reason are also sometimes considered "vertical clouds."

CUMULUS (CU) [CUE-MYU-LUSS]

Cumulus clouds are quite easy to recognize. Formed on humid days, they look like white or light-gray cotton puffballs of various shapes set against the blue sky. They are typically about a half-mile wide and their edges are clearly defined.

Cumulus can be distinguished from **stratocumulus** because cumulus clouds exist singly while stratocumulus clouds exist in groups or rows. And while cumulus clouds have rounded tops, stratocumulus clouds have relatively flat tops.

Cumulus clouds are produced by convection, the rising of pockets of warm air. This occurs as the sun warms the ground and the layer of the air above it. Cumulus clouds usually begin forming in the morning and grow throughout the day. They reach their tallest point at the warmest time of day, which is generally mid-afternoon. In the evening, they begin to dissipate.

Cumulus clouds seen from an airplane.

Cumulus clouds normally form only over warm surfaces. This fact is clearly demonstrated when cumulus clouds form over a shoreline, but not above the adjacent body of cold water. A line of cumulus clouds, known as a "cloud street," represents a boundary between warm and cold surfaces.

As long as the atmosphere is **unstable** (the ascending **air parcel** is warmer than the ambient air) at the height of the cloud base, the cumulus cloud will continue to develop vertically. The top of a cumulus cloud indicates the limit of rising air. Cumulus clouds typically grow to only moderate heights and are associated with fair weather.

When the air is particularly unstable and strong convection occurs, a cumulus cloud can reach great heights. As it surges upward, it passes through the intermediate stage of **Cumulus mediocris** and then may become **Cumulus congestus,** in which it is shaped like a head of cauliflower. During this stage, cumulus clouds grow wider and often run into one another, forming a line of towering rainclouds. If the vertical growth of a Cumulus congestus continues, it will evolve into a cumulonimbus, or thunderstorm cloud.

CUMULONIMBUS (CB) [CUE-MYU-LOW-NIM-BUS]

While the dark base of a cumulonimbus can form as low as 1,000 feet (300 meters) above ground, its top may reach 39,000 feet (12 kilo-

Cumulus mediocris clouds dot the sky in eastern Colorado.

meters), which is well into the upper reaches of the **troposphere.** In the tropics and subtropics, the top of the largest species of thunderstorm clouds, **Cumulonimbus incus,** can surge beyond the troposphere and into the **stratosphere,** up to 60,000 feet (18 kilometers).

A cumulonimbus cloud will keep growing taller as long as both convection and atmospheric instability persist. The atmosphere is considered unstable when the temperature of the surrounding air drops with increasing altitude, at a faster-than-average rate. And, on average, air temperature drops 3.6°F for every 1,000 feet (6.5° per kilometer) you ascend. For more information, see section on air stability and vertical motion in "What Is Weather?" on page 58.

If a cumulonimbus cloud extends into the stratosphere, it will encounter a reversal in the cooling trend: Temperature in the stratosphere rises with altitude. This change brings a halt to the cloud's vertical growth. If the **updraft**s continue within the cloud, it will grow outward. Ice crystals at its top will then be sheared off by the **jet stream,** and fan outward into a wedge-shaped mass, forming cumulonimbus incus. This cloud is so-named because its top is similar in appearance to a blacksmith's anvil, the Latin name for which is *incus*. Cumulonimbus incus clouds may appear singly or in ominous-looking rows called **squall lines.**

The classic cumulonimbus clouds with an anvil-like top.

Approximate Height of Cloud Bases Above the Surface for Various Locations			
Cloud Group	Tropical Region	Temperate Region	Polar Region
High	6,000 to 18,000 m (20,000 to 60,000 ft)	5,000 to 13,000 m (16,000 to 43,000 ft)	3,000 to 8,000 m (10,000 to 26,000 ft)
Middle	2,000 to 8,000 m (6,500 to 26,000 ft)	2,000 to 7,000 m (6,500 to 23,000 ft)	2,000 to 4,000 m (6,500 to 13,000 ft)
Low	surface to 2,000 m (0 to 6,500 ft)	surface to 2,000 m (0 to 6,500 ft)	surface to 2,000 m (0 to 6,500 ft)

Ice that shears off the top of this cloud's anvil may form layers of **cirrus** and **cirrostratus** clouds that cover an area hundreds of miles downwind. For this reason, cumulonimbus is also referred to as a "cloud factory."

The lower portions of a cumulonimbus cloud contain liquid water, the middle portions contain both water and ice, and the top is made entirely of ice crystals. Therefore, one cloud can simultaneously produce different forms of **precipitation,** including rain, snow, and **hail,** in great quantities.

A cumulonimbus cloud is a giant storehouse of energy. Within it are powerful updrafts and **downdraft**s of wind, blowing at speeds greater than 55 mph (88 kph). **Thunder, lightning,** and **tornadoes** all may accompany storms produced by cumulonimbus clouds.

For more information on cloud types see:

"Cloud Catalog." Dept. of Atmospheric Sciences, University of Illinois at Urbana-Champaign. [Online] Available http://covis.atmos.uiuc.edu/guide/clouds/ html/cloud.home.html

Schaefer, Vincent J. and John A. Day. *A Field Guide to the Atmosphere.* Boston: Houghton Mifflin Company, 1981.

Scorer, Richard. *Clouds of the World.* Melbourne, Australia: Lothian Publishing Co., 1972.

World Meteorological Organization. *International Cloud Atlas.* Geneva, Switzerland: World Meteorological Organization, 1987.

VARIATIONS IN CLOUD BASE HEIGHTS

The bases of clouds form at different heights, in different parts of the world. The bases of middle and high clouds form at highest elevations in tropical regions (30 degrees South to 30 degrees North) and lowest elevations in the polar regions (60 degrees to 90 degrees, North and South). They form at intermediate elevations in the temperate regions (30 degrees to 60 degrees, North and South).

Specifically, the bases of middle clouds form from 6,500 to 13,000 feet (2 to 4 kilometers) in the polar regions; 6,500 feet to 23,000 feet (2 to 7 kilometers) in the temperate regions; and 6,500 to 26,000 feet (2 to 8 kilometers) in the tropical regions. The bases of high clouds form from 10,000 to 26,000 feet (3 to 8 kilometers) in the polar regions; 16,000 feet to 43,000 feet (5 to 13 kilometers) in the temperate regions; and 20,000 to 60,000 feet (6 to 18 kilometers) in the tropical regions. The base height of low clouds is unaffected by **latitude.**

These variations in cloud base height are due to temperature. Polar air is generally colder than temperate or tropical air at equal elevations throughout the **troposphere.** Thus, air cools to its **dew point** relatively close to the ground in the polar regions, whereas it must travel to greater heights before **condensation** occurs in the tropics. For instance, **cirrus** clouds, high clouds made of ice crystals, can form as low as 10,000 feet (3 kilometers) in polar regions, whereas they will form only at twice that height in the tropics.

The ranges of cloud base heights also show some variation within a given geographic region due to the season and time of day. Again, the cause of this variation is air temperature. In the winter, middle and high clouds form at lower heights than they do in summer. And cloud base height, on average, is highest in midafternoon when the air is warmest and lowest at night when the air is coldest.

CLOUD SPECIES

We have thus far examined the ten basic groups, called genera, of clouds: **stratocumulus, stratus, nimbostratus, altocumulus, altostratus, cirrus, cirrostratus, cirrocumulus, cumulus,** and **cumulonimbus.** Within each genus (singular form of genera) there are one or more species. Species are highly defined types of clouds.

According to the binomial (two-name) system of scientific nomenclature, used to identify living organisms, the name of a particular entity begins with the genus, which is always capitalized, followed by the species. These names are in Latin. For example, a red maple tree is *Acer rubrum*. *Acer* is the genus, which means "maple," and *rubrum* is the species, which means "red." In contrast, a sugar maple tree is *Acer saccharinum*.

Much can also be learned about a cloud by translating its species name from the Latin. For instance, *lenticularis* means "lens" and describes a lens-shaped cloud; *fractus* means "fractured" and describes a cloud with irregular or ragged edges; and *pileus* means "piled up" and refers to clouds with a cap-like formation on top.

Some cloud species are subdivided into varieties. One way to name a variety is to list more than one species name after the genus name. An example of this is *Cumulus congestus pileus,* a cauliflower-shaped, sprouting cumulus cloud with a smooth, cap-like cloud above it.

Species List

What follows is a list of the most widely recognized species, the translations of their Latin roots, the characteristics they describe, and to which genera (in abbreviated form) they apply.

Cumulonimbus calvus clouds boil upwards over the Nebraska prairie on a hot summer day.

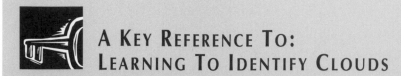

A KEY REFERENCE TO:
LEARNING TO IDENTIFY CLOUDS

Being presented with a long list of cloud types, with Latin names no less, can prove overwhelming to the novice **meteorology** enthusiast. Here are some helpful hints.

When you look up at the clouds, first look for general characteristics. Ask yourself these questions: Are the clouds flat or bumpy? Do they form a solid sheet or are they individual with distinct edges? Are they white, light-gray, or dark gray? How much of the sky is covered: Is it completely overcast, can you see patches of blue, or is it mostly blue with a few clouds? Do the clouds appear to be low to the ground or high in the sky?

By comparing your answers with the descriptions given for the ten cloud genera, you should be able to identify the genera of the clouds you're looking at. After becoming reasonably successful at this, you'll be ready to start identifying cloud species. This skill requires a familiarity with the descriptions of common species. When skywatching, it also helps to carry a good field guide or cloud atlas. These books provide pictures of clouds alongside their names and written descriptions.

- Calvus [KAL-vuss]: "bald"; upper part of a cloud is losing its rounded, cauliflower-like outline and becoming diffuse and fibrous. Applies to Cu, Cb.

- Capillatus [kap-uh-LAY-tuss]: "having hair"; cloud with **cirriform,** streaky structure on its upper edges. Applies to Cb.

- Castellanus [kas-tuh-LAY-nuss]: "castle-like" vertical extensions. Applies to Cc, Ac, Sc, Ci.

- Congestus [kon-JESS-tuss]: "congested"; upper parts piled up and sharply defined; resembles a head of cauliflower. Applies to Cu.

- Fibratus [fie-BRAY-tuss]: "fibrous," hair-like strands with no hooks or curls at the end. Applies to Ci, Cs.

- Floccus [FLOK-us]: "flock of wool"; small tufts with ragged undersides; often accompanied by virga. Applies to Cu, Ci, Cc, Ac.

- Fractus [FRAK-tuss]: "fractured," broken up, ragged edges. Applies to St, Ci, Cu (it is used as a prefix in the case of Cu: "fractocumulus").

- Humilis [HUE-muh-liss]: "humble, lowly"; small, flattened appearance. Applies to Cu.

- Incus [ING-kuss]: "**anvil**," or fan-shaped; spreading, smooth or fibrous mass at the top of a cloud. Applies to Cb.

- Intortis [in-TOR-tiss]: "intertwined"; entangled, fibrous strands. Applies to Ci.

- Lenticularis [len-tik-yuh-LAIR-iss]: "lens-shaped"; elongated, or almond-shaped with well-defined outlines. Applies to Cs, Cc, Ac, Sc.

- Mammatus [muh-MAT-tuss]: "breast, udder"; pouches of water droplets that hang from the underside of a cloud. Applies to Cb, Ci, Cc, Ac, As, Sc.

- Mediocris [me-dee-OH-kriss]: "mediocre"; moderate vertical development with lumpy tops. Applies to Cu.

- Nebulosus [neb-yuh-LOH-suss]: "nebulous"; thin, hazy veil. Applies to Cs, As, St.

- Pileus [PIE-lee-us]: "felt cap"; small cap- or hood-shaped formation perched above or attached to the top of a cloud. Applies to Cu, Cb.

- Spissatus [spi-SAY-tuss]: "tightly packed"; icy formations at the top of a vertical cloud that are dense enough to block out the sun. Applies to Ci.

- Stratiformis [stra-tuh-FOR-miss]: "covering, blanket"; thick layer. Applies to Ac, Sc, Cc.

- Translucidus [trans-LOO-si-duss]: "translucent"; transparent layer covering a large part of the sky, through which the sun or moon shines. Applies to St, As.

- Uncinus [un-SIGH-nuss]: "hook-shaped"; fibers creating the pattern called "mare's tail." Applies to Ci.

- Undulatus [un-doo-LAY-tuss]: "undulating"; wave-like formation within patches, layers, or sheets of clouds. Applies to Ac, As, Cc

EXAMPLES OF COMMON SPECIES

What follows are descriptions of some common cloud species, identified by both their genus and species names.

STRATUS FRACTUS. Nicknamed "scud," this cloud type is the ragged underside of a stratus or nimbostratus that has separated from the parent cloud above it. Stratus fractus often appears before or after a rain- or snow-shower. The cloud gets its "shredded" appearance from being blown about by the wind.

STRATOCUMULUS STRATIFORMIS. This stratocumulus has puffy cloud segments that have grown together into a solid, thick, lumpy sheet. Stratocumulus stratiformis may produce precipitation heavier than a **drizzle,** which is unusual for a stratocumulus cloud.

ALTOCUMULUS UNDULATUS. Altocumulus undulatus takes the form of parallel rows of altocumulus clouds. They may appear in patches or cover most or all of the sky. Sometimes the rows are very close together and resemble the ripples created by dropping a pebble into still water.

The rows are produced by the action of two stacked vertical layers of air, each moving in a different direction. The upper layer of air is the colder of the two. The warm air then rises to the height of the upper layer and cools, causing moisture to condense from it. At the same time, the cold air descends into the warm layer, causing the water in its path to evaporate. This **evaporation** results in cloudless rows where the cold air has traveled, interspersed with cloudy rows where the warm air has traveled.

ALTOSTRATUS TRANSLUCIDUS. Altostratus translucidus is a moderately thick, featureless cloud cover that produces a visual effect known as

*Altocumulus
undulatus clouds.*

"watery sky," sometimes called "watery sun." Watery sun is when the sun looks like a bright, blurry ball set against a gray backdrop. The sun appears much as it would when viewing it through frosted glass.

A layer of Altostratus translucidus is thicker in some parts than in others. The thickest parts of this cloud may totally obscure the sun.

CIRRUS FLOCCUS. Cirrus floccus resemble small cumulus clouds, high in the sky. These delicate, woolly-looking tufts are formed when warm air continues rising past the base of a cirrus cloud, depositing **condensation** above. Falling ice crystals, which look like hazy veils, trail beneath the clouds and are blown horizontally by the wind.

CIRRUS UNCINUS. This picturesque form of high, ice-crystal cloud looks as if it were painted on the sky with fine brush strokes. Cirrus uncinus, with its series of hook-shaped filaments, has been nicknamed "mares' tails." It also has been described as "commas" in the sky.

The distinctive look of these clouds is created by the wind. The clouds develop as follows: As ice crystals within the clouds grow, the clouds become heavier and begin to descend. They are then whipped by strong winds below, sometimes **jet stream** winds, and spread horizontally across the sky. The clouds' hooked tails indicate the direction of **winds aloft.**

CUMULUS HUMILIS. These clouds are the smallest species of cumulus cloud. They look like small tufts of cotton. Cumulus humilis are formed

Cirrus uncinus clouds.

by weak **convection** currents. This pattern stands in contrast to other species of cumulus, in which convection is stronger and produces taller clouds. Another way in which Cumulus humilis is formed is during the break-up of a layer of stratocumulus.

These clouds are relatively flat on the bottom, rounded on top, and wider than they are tall. They are always associated with fair weather. Cumulus humilis clouds may grow throughout the day, as the sun heats the surface and warm air pockets continue rising. They may evolve into **Cumulus mediocris** and **Cumulus congestus** and, under the right conditions, into a cumulonimbus thunderhead.

FRACTOCUMULUS. Fractocumulus is a cumulus cloud with tattered edges. Sometimes small fragments begin to break off this cloud. The fragments may hang on the edge of the parent cloud or may separate entirely and hover nearby.

Fractocumulus often represents an intermediate step in the development of a cumulus cloud, either as it is beginning to form or beginning to dissipate. Fractocumulus may appear white or gray, depending on the sun's position in the sky and the thickness of the cloud.

UNUSUAL CLOUDS

What follows are descriptions of some unusual cloud formations. You will note that three of the following six examples (pileus, mamma-

Cumulus humilis clouds.

tus, and lenticular) have been introduced in the species list above. Each of these formations can occur in multiple genera. In the other three examples (banner, Kelvin-Helmholtz, and contrails) we will describe clouds that are formed under special conditions and are not included in our species list.

PILEUS CLOUDS

Pileus clouds, also known as "cap clouds," are smooth formations found at the top of **Cumulus congestus** or **cumulonimbus** clouds. A pileus cloud is formed by strong **updraft**s associated with a growing **cumuliform** cloud. These updrafts, which reach speeds of 20 to 30 mph (32 to 48 kph), force a parcel of air sharply upward. The **air parcel** travels along the side of the cumuliform cloud and over the top. It settles above the cloud, where the moisture within the air condenses into a flat, elongated cloud.

If the cumuliform cloud continues to grow taller it will touch the pileus cloud, making it appear that the cumuliform cloud is wearing a pileus cap.

MAMMATUS CLOUDS

These distinctive, beautiful formations are often associated with severe weather. They most commonly develop on the underside of the anvil of a mature cumulonimbus cloud. They also form infrequently underneath **altostratus, altocumulus, cirrus, cirrocumulus,** and **stratocumulus** clouds.

Mammatus clouds are round pouches of moisture. They appear in clusters, hanging down from and covering the underside of a cloud. They typically develop on a cumulonimbus cloud after the worst part of a **thunderstorm** has passed. And, contrary to popular belief, the presence of mammatus rarely signals a **tornado.** The formation of mammatus beneath cloud types other than cumulonimbus is a sign that thicker clouds and **showers** are either approaching or retreating.

Mammatus clouds are formed under the unusual conditions of warm, moist air traveling downward, a sort of "reverse-**convection**". The process works like this: When a thunderstorm cloud reaches the top (or occasionally surpasses the top) of the **troposphere,** it quits grow-

Cumulonimbus mammatus clouds advancing ahead of a summer evening thundershower in downtown Minneapolis, Minnesota.

ing vertically and spreads horizontally, creating an **anvil.** Pockets of warm air continue to rise to the top of the cloud and travel horizontally along the top of the anvil. Due to the large concentration of ice crystals and water droplets suspended in these pockets of air, they are heavier than the surrounding air and begin to fall.

Normally, air becomes warmer as it descends, causing the moisture within it to evaporate. However, in this case, the falling air pockets contain so much moisture that any heat gained while descending is expended in the process of **evaporation.** If more heat is lost than gained during the descent, the air pockets actually become cooler than the surrounding air. In that case, the moisture within them condenses once again. When this **condensation** occurs at the base of the anvil, it forms the structures known as mammatus clouds.

LENTICULAR CLOUDS

The appearance of **lenticular cloud**s often coincides with reports of UFO (Unidentified Flying Objects) sightings. The reason for such reports is that these clouds have a peculiar, flying-saucer shape. They often appear in groups, looking like a fleet of alien spaceships. And they remain or "hover" in the sky for extended periods.

Far from being spaceships, lenticular clouds are actually part of a class of **mountain-wave clouds,** also called orographic clouds. They are

Standing lenticular cloud saucers over the Colorado Rockies.

generated when moist wind crosses over a mountain range. As described in on pages 68–69, the wind blows along the surface of the westward (**windward**) mountain side of the mountain, over the top, and down the eastward (**leeward**) side. As a result, a wave-like pattern of winds is set into motion. That pattern continues for several miles downwind of the mountaintop (see Figure 13 on page 104).

As the air moves upward toward the crest of a wave, it cools. If it is carrying sufficient moisture, clouds will form. The air then flows downward toward the trough of the wave, during which it warms and clouds evaporate. This motion results in the formation of lenticular clouds at the wave's peaks, while clouds are absent in the troughs.

If alternating moist layers and dry layers of air exist above the mountains, these lens-shaped clouds will form one on top of another, resembling a stack of pancakes. As long as the wind continues moving through the wave at a constant rate, the clouds will remain stationary.

Lenticular clouds are a common sight over most mountain ranges. The most spectacular lenticular clouds are formed over the largest mountain ranges, such as the Himalayas, the Andes, and the Rockies.

BANNER CLOUDS

Banner clouds also belong to the class of mountain-wave clouds. They are so-named because they look like banners waving from moun-

Banner cloud streaming off a small peak near Cape Town, South Africa.

taintops. A banner cloud is also sometimes referred to as "smoking mountain." It forms at a mountain's peak and drapes down over its leeward slope. A banner cloud, like a lenticular cloud, is a product of the wave-like motion of the wind across a mountain range. The reason that a banner cloud forms specifically on a mountaintop, however, has to do with changes in **air pressure.**

A banner cloud forms because air pressure builds on the windward side and subsides on the leeward side of a mountain. The windward high-pressure area is formed by the amassing of air as it travels upward, along a mountainside. As a result, pressure drops on the windward side. Condensation (and cloud formation) occurs more readily in areas of low pressure.

The most famous banner clouds are those that often adorn the peaks of Mount Everest in the Himalayas, and the Matterhorn in the Swiss Alps.

KELVIN-HELMHOLTZ CLOUDS

Kelvin-Helmholtz clouds are cirrus clouds that look like breaking ocean waves or narrow, horizontal corkscrew spirals. They are comprised of a series of **eddies** (small parcels of air that flow in a pattern different from the general air flow). Since they dissipate within a couple of minutes of forming, they are rarely seen.

Kelvin-Helmholtz clouds are the product of a strong **wind shear.** Wind shear refers to the rate of change of wind speed, or wind direction,

A thin chain of Kelvin-Helmholtz billow clouds in the sky downwind of the Colorado Rockies.

over a set distance. The formation of Kelvin-Helmholtz clouds requires the presence of two vertical air layers of different densities that travel at different speeds. The upper layer must be the warmer and less dense of the two. Given a great enough wind shear, eddies will develop where the two air layers meet.

Kelvin-Helmholtz clouds were named for Scottish physicist Baron Kelvin (1824–1907) and German physicist Hermann von Helmholtz (1821–1894), the two scientists who were the first to describe this pattern of eddies in fluids in the late nineteenth century.

CONTRAILS

Contrails are the only cloud type covered in this chapter that are not naturally occurring. These clouds are cirrus-like markings spread across the sky by aircraft flying at 16,500 feet (5 kilometer) or higher. "Contrails" is an abbreviation for "condensation trails."

A contrail is the frozen trail of water droplets emitted by an aircraft's exhaust. At high levels of the troposphere, or low levels of the **stratosphere** where large aircraft travel, the air temperature is typically below -68°F (-38°C). At this temperature water droplets freeze within seconds, appearing white against the blue sky.

When the surrounding air is relatively dry, these artificial clouds are thin, dissipate quickly, and are generally not visible from the ground.

Jet plane contrails.

Contrails formed in air with a high relative humidity, however, are thicker than their dry-air counterparts. They may remain visible in the sky for a half-hour or more, particularly if winds are light. During this time, they may spread apart, forming a sheet-like cloud.

A thick, persistent contrail is a sign of moisture in the upper air. This sign is often the first clue that a **frontal system** is approaching.

CLOUD IDENTIFICATION AND FORECASTING

Certain types of clouds, and especially sequences of clouds that develop over time, are reliable indicators of weather to come. Their usefulness for forecasting is greatly improved when wind direction is also considered. Once you have a familiarity with the basic cloud types, all it takes is regular observations of the sky to predict when the weather will be fair, wet, or stormy, as well as whether the air will become warmer or colder.

FAIR- AND FOUL-WEATHER CLOUDS

In the discussions of high, middle, and low clouds earlier in this chapter, we described which types of **precipitation,** if any, are associated with each cloud genus. What follows is a summary of the weather implications of the major cloud types.

Our discussion begins with the fairest-weather clouds: high clouds. These are **cirriform** clouds composed of ice crystals. They rarely pro-

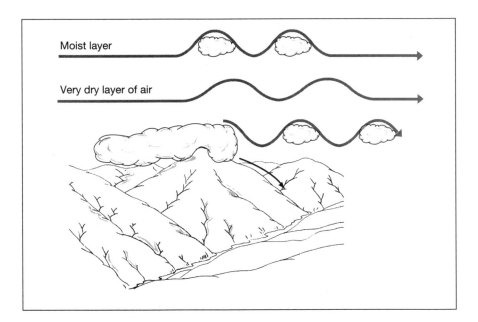

Figure 13:
Mountain-wave clouds.

duce precipitation that reaches the ground. When rain or snow does fall from these clouds, it usually takes the form of **virga,** or **fall streaks,** that evaporates as it falls.

When **cirrus** clouds thicken, however, they often represent the leading edge of a **frontal system,** usually a **warm front.** If this is the case, you can expect to see the formation of progressively lower layers of clouds and precipitation within the next twenty-four hours.

Next comes the middle clouds: **altostratus** and **altocumulus.** These clouds often form in advance of a storm. Only when they exist in thick layers will these clouds yield precipitation. The presence of Altocumulus castellanus, in the morning on a warm, humid day signifies the likelihood of afternoon **thunderstorm**s.

Low clouds are the most likely to produce steady rain or snow. **Stratus** may do nothing more than hang in the air like a gloomy, gray blanket, or it may yield light precipitation that sometimes lasts for days. A thick layer of **stratocumulus,** which is often the leading edge of a **cold front,** may bring light **drizzle** or snow. The rainiest of the low clouds is **nimbostratus,** which often produces continuous, light-to-heavy precipitation for longer than twelve hours.

The final category, vertical clouds, can do just about anything. They range from **Cumulus humilis,** the fairest of all fair-weather clouds, to **Cumulonimbus incus,** the king of the thunderstorm clouds. The degree

Altocumulus castellanus clouds.

of raininess or snowiness of these clouds depends on their degree of vertical development: the taller the cloud, the more likely that it will produce precipitation. When **cumuliform** clouds yield precipitation, it is usually localized, heavy, and short-lived.

WIND DIRECTION

Once you have identified the types of clouds in the sky, the next step in predicting the weather is to determine the direction of the surface winds. It is also important to note if, and how, the winds are shifting. Wind direction is important because the wind carries along the moisture that produces clouds and precipitation. For this reason, a change in the wind direction usually signals a change in the weather.

While we go into more detail about the role of wind direction in the chapter on "Forecasting," we present here a few rules of thumb regarding wind direction and weather prediction. Recall that "wind direction" is the direction from which the wind is coming, as opposed to the direction in which it is heading. For instance, a "west wind" is one coming out of the west.

- Foul weather is more likely when the winds are coming from the northeast, east, and south. Fair weather is more likely when the winds are coming from the northwest, west, and southwest.

- The following wind shift under a cloudy sky is important because it signals the approach of a line of thunderstorm clouds, known as a **squall line**: Winds shift from southwest to southeast, or from northwest to northeast.

- When winds shift back and forth between southwest and southeast, rain clouds and rain may be on the way. This pattern holds true even if skies are presently clear.

- Consider the case where rain is falling in the morning. If winds are coming from northeast to south and then shift westward, the rain will be over soon.

CLOUD SEQUENCES AND FRONTS

The first sign of an approaching cold front or warm front is that cirriform clouds appear high in the sky. Next come middle clouds, then low clouds. These clouds become progressively darker, eventually bringing precipitation. Once the front passes, the sky clears. The specifics of this general sequence of events are different for cold fronts than they are for warm fronts.

WEATHER REPORT:
KEEP A CLOUD JOURNAL

Try your hand at forecasting by the clouds! Each morning and evening for a week, make a sketch of the clouds you see and attempt to identify them by genus and species. For each journal entry, make predictions about which types of clouds will appear next, as well as whether or not it will rain or snow. Your predictions should be based on the sequence of cloud types that have appeared since the start of your journal. For each entry, note whether your previous prediction came true.

COLD FRONTS. A cold front, the leading edge of a relatively cold **air mass,** advances more quickly than does a warm front. It generally takes five to seven days to pass completely through an area. The first sign of a cold front is the appearance cirrus clouds, which remain in the sky for as long as several days.

After that, one can expect the development of any of a number of sequences of clouds. This pattern depends on the speed with which the front is moving. In general, however, the next type of cloud to form is **cirrocumulus,** followed by either altocumulus or altostratus. Then comes a layer of stratocumulus which becomes progressively thicker. Rain clouds, nimbostratus or **cumulonimbus,** are next on the scene.

The intensity of precipitation brought by the rain clouds depends on the strength of the **front.** The strength of the front, in turn, is determined by the contrast in temperature between the two air masses: the colder air mass being ushered in by the cold front and the warmer air mass that is being displaced. As we learned in the chapter "What Is Weather?" storms are fueled by the contrast of warm and cold air. The greater the temperature difference, the more severe the storm.

Thus, the final stage of a cold front's passage through an area can be marked by anything from an overcast sky and drizzle to a series of two or three thunderstorms. When the front has passed, blue skies and colder air remain.

WARM FRONTS. A warm front moves along more slowly than a cold front and is much gentler in its approach. Whereas a cold front pushes its way into a warm air mass, thrusting the warm air above it, a warm front overtakes a cold air mass by gliding above the cold air and nudging it along. The upper, leading edge of a warm front can arrive at a given location up to 1,000 miles (1,600 kilometers) and several days before its base arrives.

Because a warm front moves so slowly, its leading edge produces an extensive sequence of cloud types. Initially there are wispy cirrus clouds. These spread out across the sky into Cirrus spissatus. Next comes a layer of either rippled cirrocumulus (called "mackerel sky") or **cirrostratus.** After that we see the middle clouds: altostratus followed by altocumulus. As moisture continues to condense at lower levels, stratocumulus and sometimes stratus appear.

As the base of the warm front approaches, rain clouds—nimbostratus or, infrequently, cumulonimbus—form. Whereas the precipitation associated with a warm front is usually lighter than that associated with a cold front, it can last for several days, and it may be heavy at times. When the front has passed completely, the sky clears and the temperature rises.

For more information on clouds and forecasting, see:

Rubin, Louis D. and Jim Duncan. *The Weather Wizard's Cloud Book.* Chapel Hill, NC: Algonquin Books of Chapel Hill, 1989.

FOG

Fog is a cloud that forms near or on the ground. Like the clouds above, it is formed when water vapor condenses in the air so that the moisture becomes visible. In temperate regions, fog is composed of water droplets. In polar and arctic regions, fog may be composed of ice crystals.

Fog production differs from cloud production in one significant way: While a cloud is formed as air rises and cools to the **dew point,** fog is formed within surface-level air. That air is either cooled to the dew point by contact with a cold surface or is brought to the **saturation point** when water vapor is added to the air by **evaporation.**

Condensation that takes place directly on the ground takes the form of **dew** or **frost.** For a discussion of dew and frost, as well as cloud formation, see the "What Is Weather?" chapter.

Fog is technically defined as condensation in the air that restricts visibility to a bit more than 1 kilometer. If water has condensed in the low-lying air yet visibility is greater than 1 kilometer, the condition is defined as **mist.**

There are several varieties of fog, each of which is formed under a particular set of circumstances. In this chapter we will examine these different fog types.

RADIATION FOG

Radiation fog is the fog that forms after sunset on clear summer nights when a gentle breeze is blowing. A moist layer of air exists at Earth's surface and drier air lies above. Radiation fog is named for the process that drives it: radiation. **Radiational cooling** is the loss of heat from the ground, upward into the atmosphere. When clouds are present, they act as a blanket, trapping heat and reflecting it back to the ground. However, on cloudless nights, there is nothing to prevent rapid heat loss.

As the ground cools, the layer of air above it also cools. It accomplishes this via **conduction,** the transfer of heat from one molecule to another. Specifically, the low-lying air transfers heat to the cool ground. The ground then quickly radiates that heat away. If the surface layer of air cools to the dew point, the water vapor within it will condense and form a fog, anywhere from 3 to 1,000 feet (1 to 300 meters) deep. Since the surface layer of air is cooler than the layer of air above it, the surface air (and hence the fog) can not rise.

A light wind of less than 5 mph (8 kph) promotes the circulation of the lowest layer of air, bringing all of it in contact with the cold surface. In this way the entire layer of air loses heat and will cool to the dew point. If the winds are calm, only the very bottom of the surface air layer will come in contact with the ground. In that case, rather than producing radiation fog, moisture will either condense in a very shallow (less than 2 feet) layer of air, forming **ground fog,** or it will condense only on the ground, forming dew or frost.

Stronger winds also hinder the formation of radiation fog. Stronger

A northern Ohio highway is partially immersed in a thin layer of radiation fog just after sunrise.

winds bring about the mixing of surface air with warmer, drier layers of air above it. This either prevents the surface air from cooling to the dew point or, if the air does reach the dew point and fog develops, the wind rapidly disperses the fog.

Valley fog is radiation fog that forms in valleys. It may develop into a layer over 1,500 feet (450 meters) thick. Radiation fog forms in low-lying areas because of two factors. In the first place, cold air (in this case, air that has undergone radiational cooling) is heavier than warm air and sinks. In the second place, valleys often contain rivers which increase the amount of moisture in low-lying air.

In most cases, radiation fog evaporates within a few hours after sunrise, after the air and ground have warmed up. It typically reveals clear skies, since the absence of clouds was required for the formation of fog. Sometimes, however, the fog is so thick that it effectively blocks the sunlight from reaching the ground, and the ground remains cold. In such cases, which usually occur in winter, the fog may persist all day.

Radiation fog is most likely to form during long nights, when the surface air has more time to cool to its dew point. Thus, this type of fog is seen most commonly during late fall, winter, and early spring. Visibility in thick radiation fog may be reduced to as little as 10 feet (3 meters).

Ground fog forming in the early evening hours.

ADVECTION FOG

The process by which **advection fog** is formed is advection: the horizontal movement of air. In contrast to **radiation fog,** in which a layer of air is cooled as the ground radiates away heat, **advection fog** forms when a warm, moist layer of air crosses over a cold surface. The newly arrived air loses heat to the cold surface below by **conduction,** which lowers the air temperature. Once the air cools to the **dew point,** fog is formed. While it bears a resemblance to radiation fog, the two can be told apart because advection fog moves with the wind-blown warm air mass whereas radiation fog is stationary. In addition, while radiation fog usually forms at night, advection fog may form at any time of day or night.

In the spring, advection fog results when a mild breeze passes over ground that has not yet thawed. And throughout the summer, advection fog is produced by warm, moist air blowing across a lake that remains cold, such as one of the Great Lakes.

Another example of advection fog is that formed in the winter, when warm air is carried northward. When this warm air encounters cold ground, it cools to the dew point and advection fog results. For instance, warm air from over the Gulf of Mexico may travel as far as the central United States before encountering a sufficiently cold surface for advection fog to form.

Valley fog in the rolling terrain of western Wisconsin.

Advection fog is the thickest and most persistent type of fog. It sometimes reduces visibility to 650 feet (200 meters), the point at which airports are forced to close. Advection fog can form in a layer that is very shallow to one that is 1,000 feet (300 meters) deep.

SEA FOG

Sea fog is a special form of **advection fog** that only occurs at sea and in coastal areas. It is produced by the interaction of two adjacent **ocean currents** with different temperatures. A prime example of sea fog occurs in the Atlantic Ocean off the coast of Newfoundland. There the warm Gulf Stream flows northward, parallel to the cold, southward-flowing Labrador Current. When the air that is warmed by the Gulf Stream travels over the iceberg-filled Labrador Current, it is cooled and moisture condenses, forming fog. For two out of every three summer days, the coastal region off Newfoundland is shrouded by the famous "Grand Banks fog."

This process is also responsible for the thick fog that pervades England. In that case, the warm air comes from above the Gulf Stream and blows across cooler British coastal waters.

Sea fog is also well-known to the residents of San Francisco, California, and other West Coast communities. It forms in the summer when warm air from over the Pacific Ocean is carried shoreward by westerly winds. As the air moves over the colder, coastal surface water, the air cools and fog forms. The fog is then blown inland by a **sea breeze.** This explains the fog that can often be seen rolling in past the Golden Gate Bridge on a breezy, summer day. Conversely, if a **land breeze** is blowing out to sea, it will take the fog out with it. (For more information on sea and land breezes, see "What Is Weather?" on page 67.)

As sea fog moves farther inland, it crosses over warmer ground and dissipates. The bottom of the fog layer evaporates first, revealing a layer of low-level gray clouds. As the surface temperature increases, ever-higher layers of fog evaporate until it has completely disappeared. Fog also dissipates at a given location as the air becomes progressively warmer throughout the day. For this reason, coastal areas often have fog in the morning and at night, with clear skies in the afternoon.

A thin layer of advection fog forms over a cold Lake Erie surface as warm, moist air blows offshore.

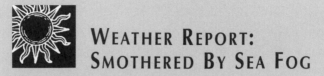

WEATHER REPORT: SMOTHERED BY SEA FOG

The town of Argentia, situated on the Avalon Peninsula of south-eastern Newfoundland, averages 206 days per year of thick fog. This makes it the foggiest place in Canada and among the foggiest places in the world. Argentia's fog is sea fog, generated by the passage of warm air over cold North Atlantic ocean water.

A similar process produces the fog at Cape Disappointment, Washington, the foggiest place in the United States. Cape Disappointment is situated at the point where the Columbia River flows into the Pacific Ocean. It is blanketed by sea fog 29 percent of the time, or about 106 days each year.

On the Atlantic Coast, the name of another foggy spot, Mistake Island, should warn you not to plan your next vacation there. This island off the coast of Maine averages 65 days of heavy sea fog each year.

Sea fog is extremely important to the vegetation of southern coastal California. Throughout the dry summers, the fog condenses on objects in its path, providing much-needed moisture to the redwood trees. The redwoods absorb moisture through their needles. Some water drips off the trees and onto the ground, where it is absorbed by the trees' shallow roots.

EVAPORATION FOG

Evaporation fog is formed in a completely different manner than any of the other types of fog discussed so far. Rather than being formed when warm air cools to the **dew point,** evaporation fog is formed when water evaporates into cool air and brings that cool air to its **saturation point.** The water may evaporate from a wide range of sources, such as a puddle, a lake, a river, an ocean, or even exhaled breath.

The reason why water molecules evaporate into **unsaturated** air has to do with the pressure exerted on water molecules. Specifically, the pressure exerted on water molecules is greater in a body of water than it is in unsaturated air. In order to equalize this pressure, water molecules leave the liquid water and enter the air. This process continues until the air becomes **saturated,** at which point water molecules experience the same amount of pressure in the air as they do in the water. After that, water molecules enter and leave the water at an equal rate. Cold air becomes saturated more quickly than warm air.

There are two main types of evaporation fog: **steam fog,** which occurs over a body of water; and **frontal fog,** which accompanies the passage of a **cold front** or a **warm front.**

STEAM FOG

The production of steam fog requires cold air to travel over a warmer body of water. Steam fog can often be seen over inland lakes and rivers in the fall, when the air is cool but the water is still warm. Water evaporates from the lake or river, saturates the cold air, and condenses into a shallow (less than 2 feet deep) layer of steam fog.

Steam fog may also be produced over a wet road or field on a sunny day. This occurs because the sun heats the water on the ground, causing it to evaporate. Steam fog continues to form in this way until the road dries. Similarly, steam fog may occur in the morning after a night of heavy **dew.** When the sun rises, it causes the dew to evaporate, saturating the layer of air above.

Steam fog rises from Lake Michigan on a sub-zero January morning.

Anyone who has taken a soak in an outdoor hot tub in the winter has noticed the "steam" rising up from the water. The same idea applies to steam fog. As the surface of cold air is warmed from below, it becomes warmer than the air above it. The warm surface layer then rises until it cools to the temperature of the surrounding air.

Steam fog occurs all year long over the thermal ponds (hot springs) in Yellowstone National Park. The reason for this pattern is that the temperature of the water is always greater than that of the air. In the winter, it is common to see steam fog over large bodies of water, such as the Great Lakes, which can take several weeks to cool to air temperature. The fog there sometimes forms in dense, rising, swirling columns known as **steam devils.**

In arctic regions, where the air is always extremely cold and dry, steam fog occurs over unfrozen waters on a large scale. Commonly called **arctic sea smoke,** this form of steam fog is patchy and wispy in appearance.

FRONTAL FOG

Frontal fog, sometimes called **precipitation fog,** is a type of evaporation fog that forms when a layer of warm air rises over a shallow layer of colder surface air. The uplift of warm air forms clouds that often yield **precipitation.** The precipitation (usually rain) that falls is warmer than

Ragged patches of upslope fog form as moist air moves up a forested mountain slope.

WEATHER REPORT: DRIVING IN FOG

Most people, when driving along poorly lit roads at night or in other conditions of reduced visibility, instinctively turn on their high-beam headlights. However, this is not a wise strategy for driving in fog. Light is scattered by fog droplets and is reflected to the driver's eyes. High-beam lights merely illuminate the fog directly ahead of the vehicle and make it difficult to see anything further.

The clearest layer of dense fog extends about a foot (about 30 centimeters) upward from the ground. Low-beam headlights point lower toward the ground than do high-beam headlights and are thus more appropriate for foggy, night-time driving. Better yet are special yellow lights called "fog lamps," used by people who frequently drive through fog. Fog lamps are installed just above the front bumper and point downward, to the area of greatest visibility.

the cold air beneath it and evaporates into the air. This raises the cold air to its saturation point and fog is produced.

This type of fog is called frontal fog because the conditions which give rise to it occur just before the arrival of a warm front or just after the passage of a cold front.

UPSLOPE FOG

Upslope fog is formed by the slow passage of a moist parcel of air up the side of a hill or mountain. As the air rises it undergoes **expansional cooling,** which is cooling due to the expansion of air over a greater area (see "What Is Weather?" on page 56). Once the air cools to the **dew point, condensation** occurs. Upslope fog generally covers a large area, sometimes hundreds of miles, and may persist for days.

Upslope fog is common in all mountain ranges. It is prevalent on the eastern slopes of the Rocky Mountains in the winter and spring. It occurs when cold air, following in the wake a **cold front,** drifts westward from the Great Plains and rides up the gentle slopes. A similar phenomena occurs in eastern Australia. There, moist air from the Tasman Sea is blown to shore and travels along the eastern slopes of the Great Dividing Range to a level where **fog** forms.

FREEZING FOG

Freezing fog is the term used to describe **fog** that develops in air that has a temperature below freezing. In most cases, freezing fog is comprised of **supercooled water** droplets. Supercooled water is water that exists in the liquid state below its freezing point. Freezing fog freezes onto any solid surface it comes in contact with, such as trees, telephone poles, cars, and roadways.

When freezing fog encounters a surface, it deposits a layer of **frost** called **rime.** Rime is not crystalline like true frost, which is called **hoar frost.** Rather, it is ice that contains trapped air, giving it a whitish appearance. Rime often persists long after the fog has cleared. It creates extremely hazardous driving conditions and is nearly impossible to walk on without slipping.

In very cold air, at temperatures below -22°F (-30°C), water droplets in freezing fog will freeze into ice crystals, becoming **ice fog.**

Rime covers fence wires after a cold fog.

One way in which ice fog is formed is from the water vapor released by the breathing of a herd of caribou or reindeer. Another way it is formed is from the passage of moist, marine air over an icy surface.

Ice fog is the least dense type of fog. It glitters in the sun, earning it the nickname **diamond dust.**

FOG STRATUS

Fog stratus, also called **high fog,** is a layer of fog that does not reach all the way to the ground. Rather, it hovers a short distance above ground. Fog stratus represents the intermediate stage through which a layer of fog (most commonly **valley fog**) passes as it dissipates.

Typically, fog forms at night. When the sun rises the next morning it begins to warm the ground. This, in turn, warms the lowest layer of air, from which the fog evaporates.

Sometimes the process of fog evaporation proceeds smoothly, from the bottom to the top of the layer, in a relatively short time. Other times, however, the fog is so thick that little sunlight penetrates it, and the air remains cold enough that fog stratus persists. Fog stratus also requires calm conditions, since winds promote mixing of the air layers and speed up **evaporation.**

A dense winter fog stratus.

Fog stratus usually clears by late morning. Occasionally, however, when clouds have moved in and inhibit the sunlight's warming of the ground, fog stratus may persist all day. A thick enough layer of fog stratus may even bring **drizzle** or snow **flurries.**

Fog stratus is common in California's Central Valley region, in the Swiss Alps, and in other mountainous regions. Fog stratus sometimes persists for weeks on end. During this period, the bottom of the fog lifts each morning, but does not entirely clear. Then, each evening, it extends back to the ground.

LOCAL WINDS

In the chapter entitled "What Is Weather?" we examined winds of a global scale: currents that circulate air around the planet. Examples of global winds include **trade winds, westerlies,** and **polar easterlies.** In this chapter we will cover **mesoscale winds,** winds that blow across areas of the surface ranging from a few miles to a hundred miles in width. Mesoscale winds are better known as **local winds** or **regional winds.** From this point onward, they will be referred to as "local winds."

A local wind can persist from several minutes to several days. They are driven either by temperature and pressure differences or variations in **topography** (shape and height of Earth's surface features). In this chapter, we will describe some general categories of local winds and the factors that give rise to them. We will also give brief descriptions of a long list of local winds that exist at various points around the world.

Alphabetical Listing of Local Winds

Name	Region it affects	Characteristics
austru	Romania	warm, dry, downhill
barih	(see shamal)	
berg	South Africa	very hot, dry
bise	southern Europe	cold, dry
blue norther	Texas	cold, snowy
bora	Croatia	cold, dry, downhill
brick fielder	southeast Australia	hot, dry
buran	central Asia	very cold
burga	Alaska	cold, snowy

Local Winds

Name	Region it affects	Characteristics
chichili	southern Algeria	hot, dry
chili	Tunisia	hot, dry
chinook	eastern side of Rocky Mts.	warm, dry, downhill
Columbia Gorge	northwest coast of U.S.	cold, dry, downhill
derecho	U.S. Plains States & Midwest	strong, stormy
Doctor, the	western Australia	refreshing sea breeze
dust devil	deserts; hot, flat areas	spinning dust storms
el norte	Central America	cold
foehn	Austria and Germany	warm, dry, downhill
gharbi	northeastern Mediterranean	mild, rainy
haboob	Sudan region, southwest U.S.	severe sand storm
harmattan	western Africa	mild, dry, dust storms
khamsin	Middle East	hot, dry, dust storms
kona	Hawaii	warm, rainy
leste	Morocco, Algeria	hot, dry
levanter	Mediterranean	mild, humid
leveche	southern Spain	hot, dry
mistral	southern France	cold, dry, downhill
monsoon	primarily southeast Asia	seasonal
nor'easter	northeast coast of U.S.	cold, stormy
nor'wester	New Zealand	warm, dry, downhill
pampero	Argentina, Uruguay	cold
papagayo	Central America's Pacific coast	cold
purga	central Asia	very cold, snowy
Santa Ana	southern California	warm, dry, wildfire hazard
shahali	central Sahara	hot, dry
shamal	Persian Gulf, Iraq	hot, dry
sharav	Israel	hot, dry, dust storms
simoom	Middle East	very hot, dry
sirocco	Sicily, Northern Italy	warm, humid
southerly buster	southeastern Australia	cold
tehuantepecer	Mexico's southern coast	cold
Texas norther	Texas	cold
whirlwind	(see dust devil)	
whirly	Antarctica	bitterly cold, spinning
zonda	Argentina	warm, dry, downhill

SEA AND LAND BREEZES

Sea breezes and **land breeze**s are two familiar categories of local winds that are driven by differences in temperature and **air pressure.** As we learned in the chapter "What Is Weather?" a sea breeze blows from the water to the shore. It comes as a welcome relief to coastal inhabitants on a hot day. A land breeze, in contrast, blows from the shore toward the water. Land breezes occur in the evening.

Sea breezes form on hot days because the land warms more rapidly than does the water. As a result, a low-pressure area develops over warm ground and a high-pressure area over the cooler water. A gentle wind blows across the **pressure gradient,** from the high-pressure area (over the water) to the low-pressure area (over the land). At night, the process is reversed as the land loses heat more quickly than does the water. The resultant land breeze flows from the high-pressure area, over the shore, out to the low-pressure area, over the water.

Sea breezes and land breezes are strongest over the shoreline, where temperature and pressure differences are most pronounced. Those breezes lose intensity as they travel inland or out to sea. The time of day when temperature and pressure differences are greatest is midafternoon, when land reaches its maximum temperature. Therefore, sea breezes are strongest at midafternoon. Sea breezes are generally stronger than land breezes, since temperature contrasts are greater during the day than at night.

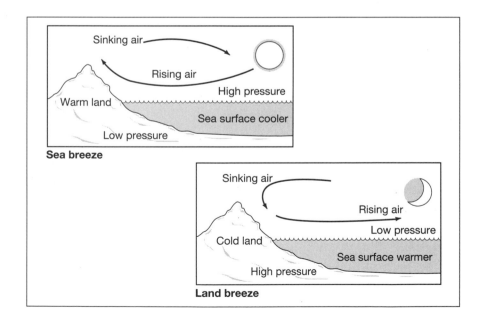

Figure 14:
Sea and land breezes.

While the strongest sea breezes blow in from over the ocean, sea breezes can also be felt on the edges of large lakes, such as the Great Lakes. **Lake breeze**s, as they are called, form in the summer (between May and August, in the **Northern Hemisphere**), on days when the land becomes warmer than the water. As a lake breeze or sea breeze travels over the land it acts like a **cold front,** thrusting the warm air above it. **Vertical clouds** and **shower**s are often produced over a stretch of land several miles inland.

The Doctor is a special name given to the sea breeze in some tropical areas, among them Perth, in western Australia. "The Doctor" is a fitting name for a wind that brings relief from the oppressive heat.

MOUNTAIN AND VALLEY BREEZES

Mountain breezes and **valley breeze**s arise from a mechanism similar to that of **sea breeze**s and **land breeze**s: different rates of surface heating and a resultant pressure differential. Valley breezes, also called **anabatic** [an-uh-BAT-ick] **wind**s (Greek for "climbing" wind), are formed during the day. The sun warms air closest to the surface of a mountain most rapidly. Air that is further above the surface, at the same altitude, warms more slowly. The warmer air hugging the surface, which is less dense than the surrounding air, travels upward along the slope. This type of wind is called a "valley breeze" because the air is flowing upward, out of the valley.

A valley breeze typically begins shortly after sunrise. It is strongest on clear, sunny days, and first develops on slopes that face east, toward the rising sun. Since east-facing slopes are also the first ones during the day to end up in the shade, the valley wind there generally stops by late afternoon.

South-facing slopes receive the greatest amount of sunlight throughout the day. Hence it is on these slopes that the strongest valley winds are found. If a valley wind contains sufficient moisture, it will produce **cumuliform** clouds and possibly **shower**s over the mountains in early afternoon.

At night, the temperature gradient between the surface air and the layer of air above it is reversed, forming a mountain breeze that blows down the slope. Once the sun goes down, the mountain surface begins losing heat to the atmosphere by **radiational cooling.** The layer of air just above the surface, which loses heat to the surface by **conduction,** also cools rapidly. This cold, dense surface air travels down the mountain and sinks into the valley. A mountain breeze is also called gravity wind or drainage wind.

Mountain breezes are usually stronger than valley winds, since at night the temperature difference is greatest between layers of air next to and farther away from the mountain. This is especially true in the winter, when the ground cools very quickly at night. A mountain breeze is one type of **katabatic** [kat-uh-BAT-ick] **wind** (Greek for "going down" wind), a wind that blows downhill.

KATABATIC WINDS

A **katabatic wind** is, technically, any wind that travels down a mountain under the force of gravity. However, the application of the term "katabatic wind" is usually reserved for downhill winds that are considerably stronger than **mountain breeze**s.

As a katabatic wind descends the mountainside, it is warmed by **compressional warming.** Compressional warming, as we learned in "What Is Weather?" occurs as an air parcel descends and is compressed by the increasing pressure of the surrounding air. That compression leads to a greater number of collisions between molecules, which causes an increase in the temperature of the air. In cases where the air is very cold when it begins its descent, the air may still be colder than the surrounding air when it reaches the base of the mountain. However, where the air was somewhat less cold to start with, the wind that flows into the lowland may actually be warmer than the **air mass** it is replacing.

Figure 15: Anabatic and katabatic winds.

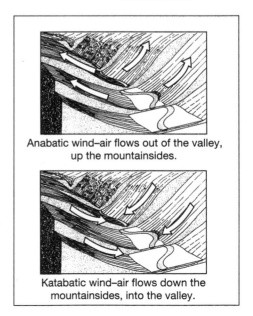

Anabatic wind–air flows out of the valley, up the mountainsides.

Katabatic wind–air flows down the mountainsides, into the valley.

Katabatic winds range in strength from gentle to **hurricane**-force. Their speed depends largely on the terrain over which they travel. For instance, the wind accelerates when it travels down long, steep slopes or is squeezed through narrow canyons and valleys.

COLD KATABATIC WINDS

Cold katabatic winds usually arise during winter or early spring on snow-capped mountains or high-elevation plateaus. The snow keeps the air above it exceedingly cold, forming a dome of high pressure just above the surface. The heavy, dense air descends along the mountainside and through the canyons. If a storm (a low-pressure system) moves into the area, the contrast in pressure between the cold surface air and the surrounding air increases, causing the wind to rush down the slopes even faster.

There are several examples of cold katabatic winds, each of which is particular to a given geographic location. One of the most famous katabatic winds is the "mistral" of southern France. Its name comes from the Latin word *magistral,* which means "master wind." This cold, dry wind comes from the north or northwest in the winter. It originates in the snowy Alps and travels down to the Gulf of Lyons on the Mediterranean Sea.

As the mistral descends through the Rhône River Valley, it is squeezed through narrow passages and picks up speed. The gusts of a mistral can exceed 100 mph (160 kph), bringing a blast of frigid air to the otherwise warm French Riviera. The mistral sometimes lowers temperatures so much that **frost** forms and endangers vineyards.

A cold, winter wind that occurs in eastern Europe is called the "bora." The bora starts out in the highlands of the former Yugoslavia and travels down to Croatia's Dalmatian Coast on the Adriatic Sea. This blustery wind travels from the north or northeast, like the mistral, and can reach speeds greater than 100 mph. The bora is, on average, even stronger than the mistral.

A "papagayo" [pa-puh-GUY-oh] is a strong, northeasterly wind that affects the Pacific coast of Central America, from Guatemala to the Gulf of Papagayo in Costa Rica. The papagayo winds are produced by a cold air mass that travels down through the Central American mountains. It brings weather that is cold and blustery, yet clear.

The "Columbia Gorge wind" is the only cold katabatic wind native to the United States. Residents of Portland, Oregon, are all too familiar with this strong wind and the cold spell it introduces. The origin of the wind is cold air that settles over the Columbia Plateau. As it sinks, the air follows the Columbia River Gorge westward through the Cascade Mountains. Upon reaching the coast, the cold Columbia Gorge wind replaces the mild coastal air.

The world's fiercest katabatic winds occur in Antarctica. There, the cold, dense air roars down the mountainsides and along the ice sheets constantly, for days and months on end. The wind averages 50 mph (80 kph) in many parts of the continent. It sometimes rages to 100 mph, generating intolerable **windchill equivalent temperature**s below -100°F (-75°C).

Experiment:
How Canyons Affect Wind Speed

In this experiment you will simulate how the wind accelerates as it squeezes through narrowing canyons or valleys. All you need is an electric fan, two pieces of cardboard or other material that can serve as walls, a pencil, and some kite string or yarn.

First, tape several 1-foot-long pieces of string or yarn to one end of the pencil. Then place the fan on a table and turn it on the lowest setting. Hold the pencil (by the end without the strings) a couple feet in front of the fan. Note how high the breeze blows the strings.

Now it's time to create your canyon walls. To do this, stand your pieces of cardboard or wood on end, on the table. Prop them up with bricks or other sturdy objects, if necessary. In order to "funnel" the wind, the distance between the walls must be greater at the end nearest the fan and smaller at the end farthest from the fan.

Turn the fan on the lowest setting again. Hold the pencil so that the end with the strings is just beyond the small opening between the "walls." The pencil should be about the same distance from the fan as it was the first time. Observe how high the strings are blown. Do you notice a difference in the intensity of the unobstructed breeze and the funneled breeze?

Warm Katabatic Winds

Warm katabatic winds are generally set in motion by a larger-scale circulation pattern, for example the movement of strong **upper-air westerlies** across a mountain range. When a **trough** of low pressure is created over the mountain's **leeward** slopes, it strengthens the high-pressure system at the mountaintop and forces air down the mountains. (For a detailed discussion of upper-air westerlies, see "What Is Weather?" on page 28.) Warm katabatic winds can also be drawn downhill by a strong **cy-**

clone (low-pressure system) or **anticyclone** (high-pressure system) located to the east of the mountains.

CHINOOK. The best-known warm katabatic wind in our part of the world is the **chinook.** The chinook is a dry wind that blows down the eastern side of the Rocky Mountains, from New Mexico to Canada, in winter or early spring. Chinooks are also common on the eastern side of the Cascades.

Chinook winds originate as cool, dry air at the top of a high mountain. The air is dry because it has released most of its moisture, forming clouds, when it ascended the mountains' **windward** side. As the air descends the leeward slopes, it undergoes compressional warming at the **dry adiabatic lapse rate.** As we explained in the chapter "What Is Weather?" (see page 56) the dry adiabatic lapse rate is the rate at which the temperature of a parcel of **unsaturated** air changes as it ascends or descends. Specifically, the air warms by 5.5°F for every 1,000 feet (10°C per 300 meters) it descends. Given that air can travel 14,000 feet or more (4,000 meters or more) down the slopes of Rockies, the warming may be considerable.

"Chinook" is an Arapaho Indian word meaning "snow eater." This name is appropriate for this wind because chinook winds bring a dramatic warming to winter-weary regions and melt snow in their path. Due to the dryness of a chinook (it may have less than 5 percent **relative humidity**), it rapidly vaporizes melted snow. A chinook can erase all signs of a foot-deep cover of snow in just a few hours.

Downslope winds off Table Mountain near Cape Town, South Africa, show both a chinook-type wall cloud and a smoke layer from brush fires burning on the flat mountain top.

WEATHER REPORT: CHINOOKS TO REMEMBER

- On January 22, 1943, in Spearfish, South Dakota, the temperature rose 49°F (29°C) in just two minutes. At 7:30 A.M. the thermometer read -4°F (-20°C) and at 7:32 A.M. it read 45°F (7°C)!

- On January 27, 1962, in Pincher Creek, Alberta, Canada, the temperature rose by 57°F (14°C) within one hour. It was -20°F (-29°C) at midnight and 37°F (3°C) at 1 A.M.

- On January 6, 1966, also in Pincher Creek, the temperature rose by 38°F (23°C) within four minutes.

- On January 7–8, 1969, outside of Boulder, Colorado, winds reached 130 mph (210 kph), with frequent gusts of more than 100 mph (160 kph). The greatest wind speed recorded within Boulder city limits was 97 mph (156 kph). That wind caused heavy property damage, including twenty-five roofs that were blown off.

Chinooks have been known to raise the temperature of an area by more than 35°F (20°C) in just one hour and by as much as 60°F (15°C) in a day. However, a chinook-induced warm spell does not mean that spring has come. The warm air can remain for several hours to days only to be displaced by cold winds from the west or the north.

There are certain dangers associated with an extended chinook-produced warm period that is followed by a return to cold weather. For instance, animals may shed their winter coats and plants may begin to germinate while it's warm. Once the cold resumes, their survival becomes questionable.

While chinooks typically reach speeds of 25 to 50 mph (40 to 80 kph), they occasionally reach speeds greater than 100 mph (160 kph). The fastest chinook gust ever recorded was nearly 150 mph (235 kph) near Boulder, Colorado, on December 4, 1978.

Violent chinooks can rip roofs off buildings and tear down trees and power lines. They whip up pebbles and debris, which can break windows and dent cars.

One warning sign of an approaching chinook is a **chinook wall cloud.** This solid bank of wispy, white clouds appears over the front range of the Rockies. A chinook wall cloud is formed as air rises along the windward slopes and moistures condenses. After this, air rapidly descends the leeward slopes.

Warm, dry winds similar to the chinook also occur in other parts of the world. Most notable is the **foehn** [pronounced FANE], also spelled "föhn," that flows down from the Alps onto the plains of Austria and Germany. In Argentina this type of wind is called zonda; in Romania it's called austru; and in the Canterbury Plains of New Zealand it's called nor'wester.

SANTA ANA WINDS. The **Santa Ana winds** are warm, dry gusting winds from the east or northeast that create a major wildfire hazard in southern California. These winds occur between the months of October and February, peaking in intensity in December. In order to be classified as "Santa Anas" by the National Weather Service, the wind must be at least 30 mph (45 kph).

Santa Ana winds originate over the elevated plateau of the Mojave Desert and wind their way through the San Gabriel and San Bernardino mountains. They gain speed as they travel through the canyons and reach tremendous speeds in the Santa Ana Canyon, for which they are named.

Smoke from massive forest fires in southern California fanned by dry Santa Ana winds.

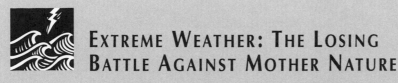

EXTREME WEATHER: THE LOSING BATTLE AGAINST MOTHER NATURE

Southern California's urban sprawl in recent decades has not stopped at the edge of wildfire- and mudslide-prone areas. Rather, homes have been and continue to be constructed in danger zones. Many foothill-dwellers have paid the price.

Since the start of southern California's building boom, Santa Ana wildfires and mudslides have caused billions of dollars in property damage and have claimed scores of lives. Following are some examples that have occurred within the present decade.

- In October 1991, wildfire invaded Oakland and Berkeley. It burned down about three thousand homes and killed twenty-five people.
- In October 1993, fifteen separate fires raged across the landscape from Ventura County to San Diego County. In all, the fires destroyed over twelve hundred buildings with damage totaling over 1 billion dollars. One month later, fires fanned by 100 mph (160 kph) winds ravaged the outskirts of Malibu.
- In October 1996, fires in Malibu and Harmony Grove destroyed over one hundred-fifty homes and burned more than forty-one thousand acres.

The winds then spill out into the foothills of the Los Angeles Basin and the San Fernando Valley.

The Santa Ana winds are generated by a high-pressure system that sits above the Great Basin, the high-altitude plateau east of the Sierra Nevadas and west of the Rockies. As this system turns clockwise, it pushes the air downward, over the edge of the high plateau, toward the lower pressure area at the coast.

Santa Ana winds blow with the force of about 40 mph (65 kph) on average, gusting to between 55 mph (90 kph) and 115 mph (185 kph). The strongest winds occur at night, in the absence of the **sea breeze.** The sea breeze blows in the opposite direction of the Santa Anas and acts as a counter force.

As the air descends, it undergoes compressional warming in the same way as the chinooks. This air originates over the desert and, therefore, is dry at the outset. Its relative humidity becomes even lower as it heats on descent. Santa Anas bring on **heat wave**s throughout southern coastal California, with temperatures reaching 100°F (38°C) or higher.

As the Santa Ana winds travel across the dry, scrubby southern California chaparral vegetation, they further dry it out and turn it into perfect brush-fire fuel. (For more information on the Mediterranean climate of southern California, see "Climate," page 468.) The Santa Anas create conditions such that a single spark can set off a fire. Once the fire begins, the winds fan the flames into an inferno. The Santa Anas are also known for changing direction rapidly, which spreads fire to new areas.

Mudslides are a secondary problem brought about by the Santa Ana winds. Mudslides often occur after wildfire has removed the vegetation and left the slopes bare. If heavy winter rains fall before seeds have germinated and new vegetation has taken hold, the top layer of soil and debris will be washed away. Mudslides occasionally inundate roadways and even destroy homes.

DESERT WINDS

Deserts are windy places, primarily because of surface heating. The temperature of dry ground on a sunny day may be exceedingly hot, in some places over 130°F (55°C). Air rises from the hot surface in a powerful **convection,** which starts surface winds blowing. Wind speeds are greatest during the hottest part of the day and during the hottest time of year.

In addition to transporting scorching heat from one place to another, desert winds may produce sandstorms. As strong winds blow across a desert, they lift up and carry along sand and dust. Sandstorms may take the form of billowing walls or clouds, or spinning whirlwinds. (For more information on deserts, see "Climate," page 462.)

SANDSTORMS AND DUST STORMS

One type of sandstorm that occurs frequently in the deserts of Sudan region of north-central Africa and occasionally in the southwestern United States is the **haboob.** This word is taken from the Arabic word *habub,* which means "blowing furiously." A haboob is a tumbling, black wall of sand that has been stirred up by cold **downdraft**s along the leading edge of a **thunderstorm** or a **cold front.** These downdrafts strike the hot, dusty ground and force the surface air, as well as the top layer of sand and dust, upward. The sand wall may rise a mile or more above the ground, sometimes all the way to the base of the **thunderstorm cloud.** Haboobs sometimes travel across distances greater than 90 miles (145 kilometers), reducing visibility to near zero.

A spinning vortex of sand and dust, called a **dust devil, whirlwind,** or, in Australia a willy-nilly, sometimes forms along the leading, cold air/warm air boundary of a haboob. More often, however, dust devils arise separately from haboobs, on clear, hot, relatively calm days. Fair-weather dust devils form over particularly warm areas, such as a desert, a plowed field, or a flat expanse of dirt or pavement. Although dust devils bear a superficial resemblance to **tornado**es, they form by different processes.

The first step in the formation of a dust devil is that hot air rises forcefully from the surface by convection, creating a low pressure area at the surface. Next, surface winds **converge** to that point of low pressure. If there are horizontal layers of wind traveling at different speeds (a phenomena called **wind shear**), rising air begins to spin around a vertical axis.

A dust devil—a spinning vortex of dust, dirt, and sand—in Kenya.

Dust devils are usually small and harmless, measuring less than 10 feet (3 meters) in diameter and less than 300 feet (90 meters) in height. They often last less than one minute. The largest dust devils reach a diameter of 100 feet (30 meters) and a height of 5,000 feet (1,500 meters) and last for twenty minutes or more. The wind speed in dust devils may exceed 85 mph (135 kph).

Every year, dust devils cause significant damage, including overturning mobile homes and tearing roofs off buildings. A large and long-lived dust devil can toss over 50 tons of dust and debris into the sky.

Sand and dust storms are also common occurrences in western Africa, due to the "harmattan" [har-ma-TAHN]. The harmattan—also spelled "harmatan," "harmetan," or "hermitan"—is a mild, dry, and dusty wind. It is an easterly or northeasterly wind that originates over the Sahara during the cool, winter months, from late November through mid-March. The harmattan blows across the continent to Africa's west coast, where, despite its dryness, it brings a welcome relief from the intense tropical heat and humidity.

The negative side of a harmattan is that it can create towering sand and dust storms, up to 20,000 feet (6,100 meters) high. Over 100 million

tons of dust are deposited into the Atlantic Ocean annually by harmattan dust storms.

WINDS OF THE SAHARA

This section covers winds that form over the Sahara Desert of northern Africa and blow across to neighboring regions. In most cases, the winds that originate in the Sahara are northerly winds, meaning they blow to the south. However, the presence of storm systems at certain locations may re-direct these winds, turning them into southerly winds. In such cases, the winds blow across the Mediterranean Sea and into southern Europe or the Middle East. These patterns, illustrated in Figure 16 on page 136, usually occur in spring or fall.

There are several names for the winds of the Sahara, depending on their point of origin and their destination.

The "leste" [LESS-tay] is a hot, dry wind that comes from Morocco or Algeria. When a storm system is present off the northwest tip of Africa, just southwest of Spain, this wind blows out over the Atlantic Ocean or the Mediterranean Sea. If the leste crosses the Mediterranean and blows onto southern Spanish shores, it is called the "leveche" [luh-VAY-chay]. The leveche, like the leste, is hot and dry. The wind picks up only a very small amount of moisture during its short trip across the water.

The **sirocco** [sir-ROCK-oh], in contrast, has a longer journey across the Mediterranean. Hence, by the time this dry, dusty southeasterly wind out of North Africa reaches Sicily and southern Italy, it has become warm and humid. The sirocco is generated when a storm system is positioned to the southwest of Italy, over the Mediterranean.

The word "sirocco" (sometimes spelled "scirocco") comes from the Arabic word *suruk,* which means "rising of the sun." In the central Sahara region, this wind is called "shahali" [SHA-ha-lee]; in Tunisia it is called "chili" [SHILL-ee]; and in southern Algeria it is called "chichili" [CHEE-chi-lee].

Another hot, dry, southerly wind originating on the Sahara, this one in Libya and Egypt, is the "khamsin" [kahm-SENE]. When a storm is present to the north-northeast, over Turkey, the khamsin blows over the northern tip of the Red Sea and into Saudi Arabia, Jordan, and Israel. The khamsin is a strong wind that pro-

Blowing sand and dust obscure a supermarket parking lot during a dust storm near Riverside, California.

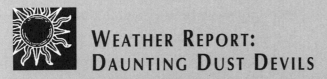

WEATHER REPORT: DAUNTING DUST DEVILS

One of the worst dust devils on record occurred in May 1995 near Minong, Wisconsin. It left a 300-yard-long (275-meter-long) path of destruction, including a damaged roof, a torn-up snow fence, and a downed power line that started a fire.

Another destructive dust devil rose up completely unannounced on a sunny day in March 1995 in upstate South Carolina. The whirlwind smashed the covered porch of a home and carried the wreckage hundreds of yards away.

In the spring of 1991, a dust devil passed right by the National Weather Service station at Albuquerque, New Mexico. The station's **anemometer** measured the wind gusts at 70 mph (110 kph).

duces large sand and dust storms. The name for this wind in Israel is the "sharav" [shahr-AHV].

The khamsin reappears regularly each year. Its name is the Arabic word for "fifty" because it blows for about fifty days continuously, starting in mid-March. The air carried by the khamsin has a temperature greater than 120°F (50°C) and a **relative humidity** of 10 percent.

The "simoom" [si-MOOM] is a dry, blustery, dust-laden wind that blows across the Sahara and the deserts of Israel, Syria, and the Arabian peninsula. It often reaches temperatures of more than 130°F (55°C), with a relative humidity less than 10 percent. Simoom, which can cause **heat stroke,** is nicknamed the "poison wind." The word "simoom" comes from the Arabic word *semum,* which means "poisoning."

"Gharbi" [GAHR-bee] is the name of a wind that originates over the Atlantic Ocean, sweeps across Morocco, and travels westward over the Mediterranean. This wind picks up dust as it crosses the desert and moisture as it crosses the water. It then deposits heavy rains on the lands of the north and east Mediterranean region. Due to the sand and dust, this **precipitation** is reddish and is called "red rain."

OTHER DESERT WINDS

The "berg" wind originates in the interior of South Africa. It blows down the mountains and out to the coast. This wind is dry, dusty, and very hot. "Berg" is an Afrikaans word meaning "mountains."

The "brick fielder" is Australia's version of a dry, dusty, very hot wind. It comes from the central desert region in the summer months and blows heat, dust, and sand toward the southeast coast.

The "shamal" [shah-MALL] is a northwesterly wind that blows throughout the Persian Gulf and the lower valley of the Tigris and Euphrates rivers in Iraq. This hot, dry, and dusty wind begins to blow suddenly, at any time of year. It typically blows for forty days continuously in June and early July, in what is known as the "great shamal" or the "forty-day shamal." At all other times of year, it generally lasts from one to five days and becomes calm at night.

"Shamal" is the Arabic word for "left-hand" or "north." Another name for this wind is "barih" [BAR-ee].

COLD WINDS

We'll begin our discussion of cold winds of the world with the "Texas norther." As its name implies, a Texas norther is a northerly wind that dips far south, bringing cold air into Texas. Texas northers (some-

Figure 16: The migrating winds of the North African Sahara region.

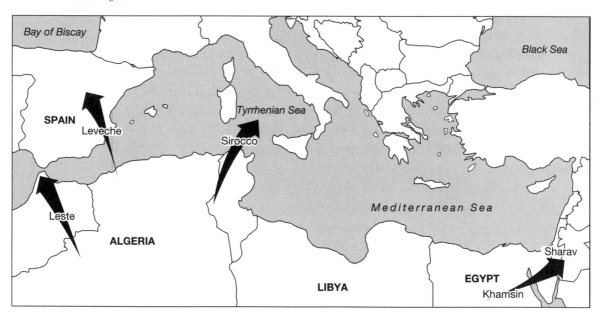

THE COMPLETE WEATHER RESOURCE

WEATHER REPORT: WINDS AND HUMAN HEALTH

Numerous local winds are thought to be responsible for declines in the mental and physical state of a region's inhabitants. While the health-wind connections in many cases are well-documented, it remains a mystery as to whether or not scientific processes are involved. What follows are examples of winds and the alleged negative effects they have on human health.

- The **chinook**s cause crabbiness, depression, and illness.
- The **sirocco** winds produce laziness and mental weakness.
- The **Santa Ana**s make people nervous, anxiety-ridden, and even homicidal.
- The **foehn**s drive people to commit suicide.

times just called "northers") usually follow in the wake of an intense winter storm traveling eastward across the United States. A Texas norther can lower the temperature in Texas by tens of degrees in just a few hours.

When a Texas norther is accompanied by snow, it is called a "blue norther." A Texas norther that continues southward and brings cold air into Central America is called an "el norte."

A **nor'easter** or "northeaster" is a strong, northeasterly wind that brings cold air to the coastal areas of New England and the mid-Atlantic states, occasionally as far south as Florida. Nor'easters are generated by storm systems in the Atlantic. These storms develop or intensify off the eastern seaboard of North America and move to the northeast along the coast. The gale-force wind that spins off the storm is often accompanied by heavy rain, snow, or sleet.

One of the most extreme cold winds is Australia's "southerly buster" (also called "southerly burster"). This violent, cold wind, which comes from the south, represents the leading edge of a **cold front.** A southerly buster can lower the temperature in southeastern Australia by as much as 36°F (2°C) in just a few minutes.

In central Asia, we find the strong, cold wind called the "buran" [boo-RAN]. This dreaded wind originates in Siberia and brings unbearably cold blasts into Russia and the eastern former-Soviet republics. When the buran is accompanied by snow, which may be heavy, it is called "purga" [POOR-guh].

A cold, snowy wind similar to Russia's purga is Alaska's "burga" [BOOR-guh], also spelled "boorga." This wind comes from the northeast and may carry sleet as well as snow.

A cold, dry wind that comes from the north or northeast and invades southern Europe is called a "bise" [BEEZ] (also spelled "bize"). This wind blows in the winter and early spring. It sometimes brings on frosts after the start of the growing season, thus endangering crops.

A "tehuantepecer" [te-WAHN-te-peck-er] is a cold, blustery, northerly wind that blows down from the Gulf of Mexico. This winter wind picks up speed as it crosses the mountains between Mexico and Guatemala. It then spills out into the Gulf of Tehuantepec, on the southern coast of Mexico, and can blow for 100 miles (160 kilometers) over the sea.

The "pampero" [pahm-PAIR-oh] is a South American wind. Similar to the Texas norther, the pampero descends from the plains and brings bitterly cold air to typically warm regions. This southwesterly wind originates in the Andes Mountains and blows across the grasslands (*pampas,* in Spanish) of Argentina and Uruguay and out to the Atlantic Coast of Brazil. The pampero is often accompanied by **thunderstorm**s and brings about a rapid drop in temperature.

The final wind to be mentioned in this section is the coldest of all: the "whirly." The whirly, alternately classified as a storm, is a small, violent squall in Antarctica. It is a rapidly spinning wind that whips up snow across an area ranging from a few yards to hundreds of yards in diameter. This windstorm usually occurs during the transition periods between the light Antarctic summer and dark Antarctic winter.

OTHER WINDS

DERECHOS

A **derecho** [day-RAY-cho] is a destructive, **hurricane**-force wind that travels in a straight line. This wind was named in 1883 by the director of the Iowa Weather Service, Gustavus Hinrichs. Hinrichs decided on the name "derecho," a Spanish word meaning "straight ahead," to underscore the difference between this wind and a **tornado,** which spins. "Tornado" is from the Spanish word *tornar* meaning "to return" or "to change."

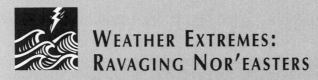

WEATHER EXTREMES: RAVAGING NOR'EASTERS

In February 1969, a storm with nor'easter winds dumped record-setting snowfalls throughout New England. In Rumford, Maine, snow accumulation totaled 70 inches (175 centimeters). There was 114 inches (290 centimeters) of snow in Mansfield, in the mountains of Vermont; and 164 inches (415 centimeters) at Pinkham Notch, in the mountains of New Hampshire.

In March 1984, a storm struck the Atlantic coast from Virginia to Maine. The shoreline was battered by waves that rose to heights of 20 feet (6 meters), along with 92 mph (148 kph) nor'easter winds. This storm destroyed beaches, homes, boardwalks, and seawalls. The damage totaled over 1 billion dollars.

Derechos received little attention in the century that followed their naming. Until the last fifteen years or so, many meteorologists had never even heard of derechos. For that reason, many derechos over the years have been wrongly classified as tornadoes. We now know that fifteen to twenty derechos occur each year, from May through August.

To be defined as a derecho, also called a "plow wind," the winds must travel faster than 58 mph (93 kph) and the path of their damage must be at least 280 miles (450 kilometers) long. Derecho winds sometimes exceed 100 mph (160 kph) and cause damage across a 150-mile-wide (240-kilometer-wide) area. Derechos are relatively long-lived. Some have swept across several states over a sixteen-hour period.

A derecho is comprised of a series of intense **downburst**s from a **squall line** or cluster of **thunderstorm**s. These thunderstorms collectively cover an area that is 75 to 300 miles (120 to 480 kilometers) wide. They act as a single storm with tremendous force. The downbursts of a derecho form when a line of thunderstorms passes over a layer of dry air that is several thousand feet above ground. As **precipitation** falls into this dry air, moisture rapidly evaporates, thus cooling the air. The cool, heavy air that is formed, assisted by the downward motion of the raindrops, then surges toward the ground. These forceful downbursts together form a derecho. They often spawn tornadoes as well.

For more information on derechos, see:

Bentley, Mace. "A Midsummer's Nightmare." *Weatherwise.* Aug./ Sept. 1996: 13–19.

MONSOONS

A "monsoon" is a seasonal wind that occurs throughout southeast Asia, along the Atlantic coastal regions of northern South America, and on the coasts of central Africa. The name "monsoon" comes from the Arabic word *mausim,* meaning "season." This wind blows throughout the summer months, bringing heavy rains and flooding to a region that has gone dry for most of the winter.

Throughout the winter, the region affected by monsoons is tilted away from the sun. As a result, the sea is warmer than the land during that time. A **land breeze** forms, and hot, dry winds from far inland are blown out toward the sea.

When spring arrives, the monsoon area moves to a position almost directly beneath the sun and the winds shift direction. The land is heated intensely, which causes surface air to rise. This air is replaced by moist winds from over the ocean, similar to a **sea breeze.** The moisture from these winds forms clouds which yield heavy rains.

The monsoons are anxiously awaited throughout southeast Asia each spring because they signal a break from the heat and the start of the

Damage to a stand of trees and a home from the passage of derecho winds in the Midwest.

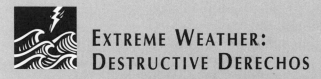

Extreme Weather: Destructive Derechos

Derechos occur most often at night, in the late spring and summer. They usually occur in the central and northern Plains States and the Midwest, and sometimes as far east as New York.

Kansas' Wichita and Sedgewick Counties fell victim to a severe derecho in June, 1990. The winds blasted through at 116 mph (186 kph), toppling trees, destroying buildings, and tearing down utility poles and power lines. The damage totaled more than $50 million.

In July 1995, a derecho blasted through New York State and southern New England in just three and a half hours. It ravaged rural upstate New York with wind gusts of up to 106 mph (170 kph), accompanied by thousands of **lightning** strikes. The wind storm knocked down tens of millions of trees across the nearly one-million acre Adirondack State Park, piling felled trees 10 to 20 feet (3 to 6 meters) high. Four people who were camping in the park were killed by the falling trees.

growing season. (For more information about monsoons, see "Climate," page 459.)

LEVANTERS

The "levanter" [li-VAN-ter] (also spelled "levante") is the most pleasant wind in the Mediterranean region. The levanter is a fresh, mild easterly or northeasterly wind that blows across the southern coast of France, the eastern coast of Spain, and through the Straits of Gibraltar. It is named for Levant, a region along eastern shores of the Mediterranean sea.

The levanter travels over the Mediterranean, which makes it humid. This often-strong wind brings overcast skies and rain. It occurs most frequently in June through October.

KONAS

Hawaii is famous for its overall pleasant weather, which is largely influenced the **trade winds.** The "kona" [KOH-nuh] winds, which usher in heavy rains and storms, stand in contrast to this trend. The konas are southwesterly winds that blow down **leeward** (the Hawaiian word for which is "kona") slopes of Hawaii's mountains, about five times each winter.

These warm, very humid winds are of moderate strength. They may produce intense storms with heavy rainfall or steady-to-light rainfall, lasting from several hours to several days.

THE WIND'S EFFECT ON SURFACES

Local winds are like sculptors, etching away at surfaces and objects standing in their path. The winds blow the sand, snow, and water, and even shape rock walls and trees. The effect of the winds can be gradual and long-term, such as where it shapes the **buttes** of the American West and the **sand dune**s of the Sahara Desert. The effect of the winds can also be much more immediate and short-term, such as where it whips water into waves and blows snow into drifts or dunes.

SAND FORMATIONS

Even a moderate desert wind can set sand in motion. A wind of about 15 mph (24 kph) is strong enough to move very small grains of sand, with diameters of about .008 inches (.2 millimeters). At speeds of

Commuters in Manila, the Philippines, wade through flood waters caused by monsoon rains when the passenger bus they were riding in stalled.

30 mph (48 kph), the wind can move grains with diameters of about .08 inches (2 millimeters). Ironically, the tiniest particles of dust and sand can not be moved directly by the wind. The reason is that a very shallow layer of calm air, extending only about .004 inches (.1 millimeters) above the ground, is unaffected by the wind. The tiny particles are stirred only when they are struck by moving particles.

When the wind blows, it sets in motion a process called **saltation,** the migration of particles along the ground and through the air. When sand particles are set in motion by the wind, they first slide along the surface. Once these particles overtake and strike other particles, some of the particles bounce into the air and are carried along by the wind. These particles, in turn, fall back to the ground and kick other particles up, into the wind. Eventually, through this process, sand can be blown across great distances.

As sand is continually carried away from a particular location, the surface level becomes lower and lower. Eventually, if all the sand and dust is removed, all that remains is hard, flat, dry ground and gravel. This type of surface is called **desert pavement.** The bare, dry floor of the Gobi Desert in Mongolia is an example of desert pavement. Desert pavements can also be formed outside of deserts. Agricultural fields, for instance, may turn to desert pavement when soil erosion is accompanied by prolonged drought.

Desert winds blow sand particles in a process called saltation.

The wind may also sculpt the sand into sand dunes. Sand dunes form when billions of sand grains accumulate in a given location. A sand dune is a mound of sand that is produced over time by a strong wind blowing in a fairly constant direction. Blowing sand comes to a halt behind obstacles, such as rocks or plants. When an accumulation of sand becomes large enough, the sand pile itself acts as an obstacle behind which blowing sand continues to gather.

The angle of a sand dune is more gradual on the **windward** side, where the wind blows strongest, and steeper on the **leeward** side, where the wind is calm by comparison. The difference in angle of incline from one side of the dune to the other results because the wind blows the sand up the windward face to the top of the dune. On reaching the top of the dune, the sand merely drops to the other side. By examining the shape of a sand dune, it is possible to tell the direction of the **prevailing winds** at the time the dune was formed.

Entire dunes are also nudged along by the wind. Sand dunes move as much as 50 feet (15 meters) a year.

Barchan [bar-KHAN] **dune**s (also called barchane, barkhan, or crescentic dunes) are formed by winds blowing in a nearly constant direction and moderate speed, across relatively flat land with only a shallow layer of sand. When viewed from above, these dunes resemble crescent moons, with the tips of the crescent pointing downwind.

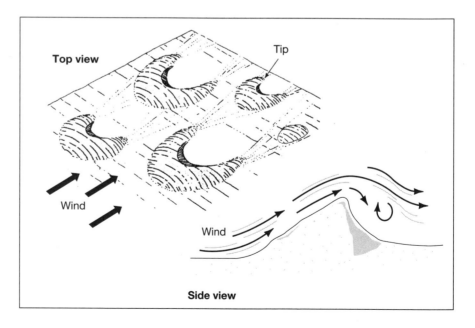

Figure 17: Barchan dunes.

If you are standing on the ground and looking at the windward face, a barchan dune looks like a convex semi-circle, with the bulge pointing towards you. If you walk around to the leeward side, the dune appears concave. The middle portion arches away from you and the tips arc around in your direction. Barchan dunes may grow as tall as a several-story building.

Where sand is more plentiful, a series of connected barchan dunes may form. This structure, called **transverse dunes,** appears as tall, elongated crescents of sand running perpendicular to the prevailing winds.

Barchan dunes with very pronounced crescent shapes, that exist either singly or in connected lines, are called **seif** [pronounced SAFE] **dune**s. These dunes are very steep; the crest of a seif dune forms a sharp ridge.

"Seif" is an Arabic word meaning "sword." These dunes are so-named because their shape resembles the curved blade of a sword. The seif dunes of Algeria and Iran reach up to 650 feet (197 meters) in height. When seifs exist in a series, they form a meandering pattern that is caused by shifting winds.

Sand ripples are wavy designs formed by the motion of sand along the surface of a sand dune. The ripples run in a direction perpendicular to the wind. Like a sand dune itself, sand ripples have a more gradual incline on the windward side of the dune and a steeper incline on the leeward side. The direction of the sand ripples changes whenever the wind changes direction.

SCULPTED OBJECTS

Another consequence of wind and wind-blown sand is the eroding and shaping of solid objects. Rocks that have been sculpted by these forces are called **ventifact**s. Ventifacts include not only rocks lying on the ground, but larger structures such as boulders and canyon walls. Surface rocks, however, constitute the bulk of ventifacts. The reason for this fact is that wind-borne sand generally travels close to the ground.

Wind and blowing sand can also erode the bases of solid rock structures, such as boulders, canyons, and cliffs. The wind has the greatest effect on soft rock, such as sandstone. The windward side of a boulder may be rough and pitted, even notched, while its leeward side is relatively smooth. Sometimes wind-blown sand has the effect of polishing rocks. This effect occurs most often in areas prone to sandstorms, where billions of sand grains batter the rocky surfaces.

Utah's Goblin Valley abounds with ventifacts. The sandstone formations there, made of alternating hard and soft layers, have been sculpted into strange and beautiful shapes by the wind. One particular type of ventifact found in Goblin Valley is the "mushroom rock." Mushroom rocks form from boulders, the lower portions of which are made of soft sandstone and the upper portions of which are made of hard sandstone. The wind erodes the soft portion at a much faster rate than the hard portion. Thus, these rocks look like mushrooms, with large heads of hard sandstone sitting atop skinny stems of soft sandstone.

One of the world's largest and most magnificent collections of ventifacts is found in Bryce Canyon, Utah. There, the wind (as well as water) has battered the tops of tall, layered rock formations. The erosion of the outer layers has created a breathtaking array of pointy stone spires.

Rock is not the only material to be shaped by wind-blown sand. Telephone poles, trees, and cars can also be sculpted in the desert. Because of the constant beating by wind-blown sand on lower portions of telephone poles, the poles become narrower at the base than they are higher up.

In locations where winds are strong and the direction is constant, one will find trees that have been twisted so that every branch points downwind. And strong desert winds can completely erode a car's paint, as well as pitting or even shattering the windshield.

SNOW FORMATIONS

Another medium sculpted by the wind is snow. Snow can be blown into large drifts called **snow dune**s that are similar to sand dunes. Snow dunes form when a strong wind comes along after snow has fallen on a flat landscape. The wind carries the snow until it meets a barrier, where it deposits the snow. In the Plains States, when snow falls on fields and is blown away, the first obstacles it meets are typically in populated areas. For this reason, snow accumulation may be negligible in the countryside at the same time that there are several inches in town.

Gentler winds form ripples in the snow, rather than blowing it away. **Snow ripples,** similar to sand ripples, are long wavelike patterns that run perpendicular to the direction of the wind.

Snow ripples in Antarctica and other very cold places are called **sastrugi** [SASS-truh-ghee]. These patterns form when the wind blows from the same direction for several days. Sastrugi freeze solid and can remain

WEATHER REPORT: SNOW FENCES

Snow fences are devices that slow down winds and reduce the blowing and drifting of snow. They are erected primarily in two areas: in fields and along highways. The purpose of snow fences in fields is to prevent the wind from stripping the ground of snow. A blanket of snow protects the soil by insulating it against bitter cold temperatures. The snow also provides much-needed moisture when it melts.

The purpose of snow fences along a highway is to reduce the amount of snow that blows across or piles up on the road. As the wind whips across a clearing, it picks up snow. When this snow-laden wind hits a snow fence, its speed is reduced. A slower wind will deposit its snow, and at the same time will pick up very little new snow. The snow that's deposited forms a gradual drift on the other (downwind) side of the snow fence.

A snow fence must be placed far enough from the road so that most of the snow gets deposited between the fence and the road, with as little snow as possible reaching the road. The rule of thumb is that snow will accumulate downwind of the fence for a distance approximately ten times the height of the fence. Thus, if a fence is 10 feet (3 meters) high, it should be placed at least 100 feet (30 meters) from the road.

for a long time. The singular form of "sastrugi" is "sastruga," which comes from the Russian word *zastruga,* meaning "wind-made furrow."

WATER FORMATIONS

In addition to sand and snow, the surface of water is also shaped by the winds. However, only one pattern can be created on the water's surface: waves. Wind-driven waves are technically known as **wind waves.** While the wind is the most common cause of surface waves, it is not the

WEATHER REPORT: THE WINDIEST PLACES IN THE WORLD

The following list takes into account only *recorded* wind speeds. Faster winds have probably occurred at other locations, but were not recorded.

Antarctica is home to the world's windiest location, Commonwealth Bay. This bay is situated on the coast of Eastern Adelie Land and West King George Land. It is on the Indian Ocean side of the continent, opposite Australia.

The wind at Commonwealth Bay was measured in 1951 by a team of French scientists who established a base there. They clocked the cold **katabatic** winds at 40 mph (65 kph) on average, for the year. The highest monthly average winds were 65 mph (105 kph), in March. The highest average winds in a twenty-four-hour period were 108 mph (174 kph), on March 21–22. The winds regularly gusted to over 200 mph (320 kph).

The windiest place in the United States is Mount Washington, New Hampshire. The Mount Washington Observatory, located at an altitude of 6,288 feet (1,915 meters), recorded a wind gust of 231 mph (371 kph) on April 12, 1934. Subsequently, there have been frequent gusts up to 220 mph (355 kph) recorded there. Mount Washington also holds the U.S. record for the highest mean wind speed in a twenty-four-hour period. On April 12, 1932, the wind blew at an average speed of 130 mph (210 kph).

The overall windiest city in the United States is not Chicago, as you may think, but Cheyenne, Wyoming. The wind speed there, averaged throughout 1990, was 12.9 mph (20.8 kph). The second windiest city is Great Falls, Montana, with a 1990 average wind speed of 12.8 mph (20.6 kph). Chicago ranks twenty-first, with a 1990 average wind speed of 10.3 mph (16.6 kph).

only cause. Some other forces that give rise to waves include: tides, volcanic activity, and earthquakes beneath the ocean floor.

Wave height is directly proportional to wind speed. To calculate the height of waves precisely, however, you must also know the length of time for which the wind has been blowing, as well as the distance over water, or **fetch,** the wind is blowing. The longer the time and distance over which the wind blows, the taller the waves will be.

It stands to reason that the largest wind waves are generated by large, stationary storm systems. The tallest wind wave ever recorded was 112 feet (34 meters) high. This wave occurred during a storm on the Pacific Ocean, with winds of nearly 70 mph (112 kph), on February 7, 1933. This wave was not the tallest of all waves, however. That title is reserved for another class of waves called **tsunami**s, which are generated by submarine earthquakes. (For more information on tsunamis, see "Temperature Extremes, Floods, and Droughts," page 308.)

SOURCES

BOOKS

Ahrens, C. Donald. *Meteorology Today: An Introduction to Weather, Climate, and the Environment.* 5th ed. St. Paul, MN: West Publishing Company, 1994.

Allaby, Michael. *How the Weather Works: 100 Ways Parents and Kids Can Share the Secrets of the Atmosphere.* Pleasantville, NY: The Reader's Digest Association, Inc., 1995.

Allaby, Michael, ed. *Illustrated Dictionary of Science.* Rev. ed. New York: Facts on File, Inc., 1995.

Anthes, Richard A. *Meteorology.* 6th ed. New York: Macmillan Publishing Company, 1992.

Bair, Frank E., ed. *The Weather Almanac.* 6th ed. Detroit: Gale Research, 1992.

Bair, Frank E., ed. *Weather of U.S. Cities.* 4th ed. Detroit: Gale Research, 1992.

Burroughs, William J. and Bob Crowder, et. al. *Nature Company Guides: Weather.* New York: Time Life Books, 1996.

Burroughs, William James. *Watching the World's Weather.* Cambridge, England: Cambridge University Press, 1991.

Carnegie Library of Pittsburgh, Science and Technology Department. *The Handy Science Answer Book.* Detroit: Visible Ink Press, 1994.

Christian, Spencer. *Spencer Christian's Weather Book.* New York: Prentice Hall, 1993.

Climates of the States. 3rd ed. Detroit: Gale Research, 1985.

Cosgrove, Brian. *Eyewitness Books: Weather.* New York: Alfred A. Knopf, 1991.

Davies, J. K. *Space Exploration.* Edinburgh, Scotland: W & R Chambers Ltd., 1992.

Day, John A. and Vincent Schaefer. *Peterson First Guide to Clouds and Weather.* New York: Houghton Mifflin Company, 1991.

DeMillo, Rob. *How Weather Works.* Emeryville, CA: Ziff-Davis Press, 1994.

Dolan, Edward F. *The Old Farmer's Almanac: Book of Weather Lore.* Dublin, NH: Yankee Publishing Inc., 1988.

Dunlop, S. and F. Wilson. *The Larousse Guide to Weather Forecasting.* New York: Larousse and Co. Inc., 1982.

Engelbert, Phillis. *Astronomy and Space: From the Big Bang to the Big Crunch.* Detroit: U•X•L, 1997.

Sources

Fields, Alan. *Partly Sunny: The Weather Junkie's Guide to Outsmarting the Weather*. Boulder, CO: Windsor Peak Press, 1995.

Fishman, Jack and Robert Kalish. *The Weather Revolution: Innovations and Imminent Breakthroughs in Accurate Forecasting*. New York: Plenum Press, 1994.

Gaskell, T. F. and Martin Morris. *World Climate: The Weather, the Environment and Man*. New York: Thames and Hudson, 1979.

Graedel, Thomas E. and Paul J. Crutzen. *Atmosphere, Climate, and Change*. New York: Scientific American Library. 1995.

Greenler, Robert. *Rainbows, Halos, and Glories*. Cambridge, England: Cambridge University Press, 1980.

Hardy, Ralph. *Teach Yourself Weather*. Lincolnwood, IL: NTC Publishing Group, 1996.

Hardy, Ralph, et al. *The Weather Book*. Boston: Little, Brown and Company, 1982.

Hatherton, Trevor, ed. *Antarctica: The Ross Sea Region*. Wellington, New Zealand: DSIR Publishing, 1990.

Henson, Robert. *Television Weathercasting: A History*. Jefferson, NC: McFarland & Company, Inc., 1990.

Holford, Ingrid. *Weather Facts & Feats*. 2nd ed. Middlesex, England: Guinness Superlatives Limited, 1982.

Kahl, Jonathan D. W. *Weather Watch: Forecasting the Weather*. Minneapolis: Lerner Publications Company, 1996.

Keen, Richard A. *Michigan Weather*. Helena, MT: American & World Geographic Publishing, 1993.

Lamb, H. H. *Climate, History and the Modern World*. 2nd ed. London, England: Routledge, 1995.

Lambert, David and Ralph Hardy. *Weather and Its Work*. London, England: Orbis Publishing Limited, 1984.

Lampton, Christopher. *Meteorology: An Introduction*. New York: Franklin Watts, 1981.

Leggett, Jeremy, ed. *Global Warming: The Greenpeace Report*. Oxford, England: Oxford University Press, 1990.

Lockhardt, Gary. *The Weather Companion: An Album of Meteorological History, Science, Legend, and Folklore*. New York: John Wiley & Sons, Inc., 1988.

Ludlam, F. H. and R. S. Scorer. *Cloud Study: A Pictorial Guide*. London, England: John Murray, 1957.

Ludlum, David M. *The Weather Factor*. Boston: Houghton Mifflin Company, 1984.

Lutgens, Frederick K. and Edward J. Tarbuck. *The Atmosphere: An Introduction to Meteorology*. 5th ed. Englewood Cliffs, NJ: Prentice Hall, 1992.

Lydolph, Paul E. *The Climate of the Earth*. Lanham, MD: Rowman & Littlefield Publishers, Inc., 1985.

Lynch, David K. and William Livingston. *Color and Light in Nature*. Cambridge, England: Cambridge University Press, 1995.

Lyons, Walter A. *The Handy Weather Answer Book*. Detroit: Visible Ink Press, 1997.

Mason, Helen. "Tom Kudloo: Aerologist." *Great Careers for People Who Like Being Outdoors*. Detroit: U•X•L, 1993.

McPeak, William J. "Edward N. Lorenz." *Notable Twentieth-Century Scientists*. Vol. 3. Ed. Emily J. McMurray. New York: Gale Research, 1995.

McPeak, William J. "Jacob Bjerknes." *Notable Twentieth-Century Scientists*. Vol. 1. Ed. Emily J. McMurray. New York: Gale Research, 1995.

Meinel, Aden and Marjorie Meinel. *Sunsets, Twilights, and Evening Skies*. Cambridge, England: Cambridge University Press, 1983.

Mogil, H. Michael and Barbara G. Levine. *The Amateur Meteorologist: Explorations and Investigations*. New York: Franklin Watts, 1993.

Moran, Joseph M. and Lewis W. Morgan. *Essentials of Weather*. Englewood Cliffs, NJ: Prentice Hall, 1995.

Moran, Joseph M. and Lewis W. Morgan. *Meteorology: The Atmosphere and the Science of Weather*. Edina, MN: Burgess Publishing, 1986.

Naseri, Muthena and Douglas Smith. "Solar Energy." *Environmental Encyclopedia*. Cunningham, William P., et al, eds. Detroit: Gale Research, 1994.

National Research Council, Committee on Atmospheric Sciences. *Weather and Climate Modification*. Detroit: Grand River Books, 1973.

Newton, David E. *Global Warming: A Reference Handbook*. Santa Barbara, CA: ABC-CLIO, Inc., 1993.

Newton, David E. *The Ozone Dilemma: A Reference Handbook*. Santa Barbara, CA: ABC-CLIO, Inc., 1995.

Newton, David E. "Wind Energy." *Environmental Encyclopedia*. Cunningham, William P., et al, eds. Detroit: Gale Research, 1994.

Oleck, Joan. "Tetsuya Theodore Fujita." *Notable Twentieth-Century Scientists*. Vol. 2. Ed. Emily J. McMurray. New York: Gale Research, 1995.

Pine, Devera. "Carl-Gustaf Rossby." *Notable Twentieth-Century Scientists*. Vol. 3. Ed. Emily J. McMurray. New York: Gale Research, 1995.

Posey, Carl A. *The Living Earth Book of Wind & Weather*. Pleasantville, NY: The Reader's Digest Association, Inc., 1994.

Robinson, Andrew. *Earth Shock: Hurricanes, Volcanoes, Earthquakes, Tornadoes and Other Forces of Nature*. New York: Thames and Hudson, 1993.

Roth, Charles E. *The Sky Observer's Guidebook*. New York: Prentice Hall Press, 1986.

Rubin, Louis D. and Jim Duncan. *The Weather Wizard's Cloud Book*. Chapel Hill, NC: Algonquin Books of Chapel Hill, 1989.

Ryan, Martha. *Weather*. New York: Franklin Watts, 1976.

Schaefer, Vincent J. and John A. Day. *A Field Guide to the Atmosphere*. Boston: Houghton Mifflin Company, 1981.

Schneider, Stephen H., ed. *Encyclopedia of Climate and Weather*. New York: Oxford University Press, 1996.

Schwarz, Joel. "Lewis Fry Richardson." *Notable Twentieth-Century Scientists*. Vol. 3. Ed. Emily J. McMurray. New York: Gale Research, 1995.

Scorer, Richard. *Clouds of the World*. Melbourne, Australia: Lothian Publishing Co., 1972.

Scorer, Richard and Arjen Verkaik. *Spacious Skies*. Newton Abbot, England: David & Charles Publishers, 1989.

Sybil, P. Parker, ed. *McGraw-Hill Dictionary of Earth Science*. 5th ed. New York: McGraw-Hill, 1997.

Tannenbaum, Beulah and Harold E. Tannenbaum. *Making and Using Your Own Weather Station*. New York: Franklin Watts, 1989.

Travers, Bridget, ed. *The Gale Encyclopedia of Science*. 6 Volumes. New York: Gale Research, 1996.

Travers, Bridget, ed. *World of Invention*. Detroit: Gale Research, 1994.

Travers, Bridget, ed. *World of Scientific Discovery*. Detroit: Gale Research, 1994.

Sources

Trewartha, Glenn T. and Lyle H. Horn. *An Introduction to Climate.* 5th ed. New York: McGraw-Hill Book Co., 1980.

Vickery, Donald M. and James F. Fries. *Take Care of Yourself.* 6th ed. Reading, MA: Addison-Wesley Publishing Company, 1996.

Wagner, Ronald L. and Bill Adler, Jr. *The Weather Sourcebook: Your One-Stop Resource for Everything You Need to Feed Your Weather Habit.* Old Saybrook, CT: The Globe Pequot Press, 1994.

Watt, Fiona and Francis Wilson. *Weather and Climate.* London: Usborne Publishing Ltd., 1992.

Williams, Jack. *The Weather Book: An Easy-to-Understand Guide to the USA's Weather.* New York: USA Today & Vintage Books, 1992.

Witze, Alexandra. "Alfred Wegener." *Notable Twentieth-Century Scientists.* Vol. 4. Ed. Emily J. McMurray. New York: Gale Research, 1995.

World Meteorological Organization. *International Cloud Atlas.* Geneva, Switzerland: World Meteorological Organization, 1987.

ARTICLES

Addison, Doug. "Filmmaker to Storm Chasers." *Weatherwise.* June/July 1996: 29–32.

Addison, Doug. "Superstorm Success." *Weatherwise.* June/July 1995: 18–24.

Addison, Doug. "Weathercasting: Forecasts on the Fly." *Weatherwise.* August/September 1995: 8–9.

Bentley, Mace. "A Midsummer's Nightmare." *Weatherwise.* August/September 1996: 13–19.

Black, Harvey. "Heat: Air Mass Murderer." *Weatherwise.* August/September 1996: 11–12.

Black, Harvey. "Hurricanes: Satellite Enhancements." *Weatherwise.* February/March 1996: 10–11.

Brotak, Edward. "Reviews and Resources." *Weatherwise.* October/November 1996: 40–41.

Brotak, Edward, Stanley Gedzelman, and Dean Lewis. "Reviews and Resources." *Weatherwise.* December 1996/January 1997: 47.

Browne, Malcolm W. "Are Lightning Balls Spheres of Plasma?" *The New York Times.* 10 September 1996: C1, C9.

Cerveny, Randy. "From Corn Flakes to Computers: Making Weather in the Movies" *Weatherwise.* December 1996/January 1997: 35–40.

"Carolinas Clean Up the Mess Bertha Left." *The Washington Post.* 14 July 1996: A4.

Coco, Mark J. "Stalking the Green Flash!" *Weatherwise.* December 1996/January 1997: 31–34.

Corfidi, Stephen. "The Colors of Twilight." *Weatherwise.* June/July 1996: 14–19.

Darack, Ed. "Majestic Mantle: Mountain Weather Can Be a Climber's Reward." *Weatherwise.* December 1995/January 1996: 24–28.

De Wire, Elinore. "England's Great Storm." *Weatherwise.* October/November 1996: 34–38.

De Wire, Elinore. "When the Heavens Dance: The Awesome Aurora Inspire Humanity To Create Magical Metaphor." *Weatherwise.* December 1995/January 1996: 18–20.

Dickinson, Robert. "The Climate System." *Reports to the Nation on Our Changing Planet.* Washington: NOAA, Winter 1991.

Eames, Stanley B. "Project Atmosphere: Improving the Teaching of Meteorology."

Weatherwise. August/September 1992: 20–23.

Fields, Alan. "A Gift Fit for a Weather Buff: Birthday Shopping Made Easy." *Weatherwise*. December 1995/January 1996: 22–23.

Gedzelman, Stanley. "Automating the Atmosphere." *Weatherwise*. June/July 1995: 46–51.

Gedzelman, Stanley. "Beyond Bergen." *Weatherwise*. June/July 1995: 37.

Gedzelman, Stanley. "Halo Heaven: Close Encounters With Colorful Rings." *Weatherwise*. August/September 1995: 34–40.

Gedzelman, Stanley. "Mysteries in the Clouds." *Weatherwise*. June/July 1995: 55–57.

Gedzelman, Stanley. "Our Global Perspective." *Weatherwise*. June/July 1995: 63–67.

Gedzelman, Stanley. "Using Your Computer: The Power of Imitation." *Weatherwise*. April/May 1993: 36+.

Gedzelman, Stanley. "Using Your Computer: Weaving Rainbows." *Weatherwise*. August/September 1996: 42–45.

Gedzelman, Stanley and Patrick Hughes. "The New Meteorology." *Weatherwise*. June/July 1995: 26–36.

Geer, Ira W. *Increasing Weather Awarness with NOAA Weather Radio: A Guide for Elementary Schools*. Washington: GPO, 1983.

Graf, Dan. "California Crazy: West Coast Winters Are Often Far From Laid-Back When El Niño Flares Up." *Weatherwise*. December 1995/January 1996: 29–32.

Graf, Daniel, William Gartner and Paul Kocin. "Snow." *Weatherwise*. February/March 1996: 48–52.

Grenci, Lee. "When Storms Die." *Weatherwise*. June/July 1996: 48–49.

Henson, Robert. "Smells Like Rain." *Weatherwise*. April/May 1996: 29–32.

Hickcox, David H. "Temperature Extremes." *Weatherwise*. February/March 1996: 54–58.

Hill, Carolinda. "Mayday!" *Weatherwise*. June/July 1996: 25–28.

Horstmeyer, Steve. "Tilting at Wind Chills: Is Winter's Popular Index Blown Out of Proportion?" *Weatherwise*. October/November 1995: 24–28.

Hughes, Patrick. "Dust Bowl Days." *Weatherwise*. June/July 1995: 32–33.

Hughes, Patrick. "The Meteorologist in Your Life." *Weatherwise*. June/July 1995: 68–71.

Hughes, Patrick. "Probing the Sky." *Weatherwise*. June/July 1995: 52–54.

Hughes, Patrick. "Realizing the Digital Dream." *Weatherwise*. June/July 1995: 44–45.

Hughes, Patrick. "The View from Space." *Weatherwise*. June/July 1995: 60–62.

Hughes, Patrick. "Winning the War." *Weatherwise*. June/July 1995: 38–41.

Hughes, Patrick and Douglas Le Comte. "Tragedy in Chicago." *Weatherwise*. February/March 1996: 18–20.

Hughes, Patrick and Richard Wood. "Hail: The White Plague." *Weatherwise*. April/May 1993: 16–21.

Iocavelli, Debi. "Hurricanes: Eye Spy." *Weatherwise*. August/September 1996: 10–11.

Kristof, Nicholas D. "In Pacific, Growing Fear of Paradise Engulfed." *The New York Times*. 2 March 1997: 1.

Le Comte, Douglas. "Going to Extremes: 1995 Was Wild and Woolly for the U.S." *Weatherwise*. February/March 1996: 14+.

Sources

Martner, Brooks. "An Intimiate Look at Clouds." *Weatherwise*. June/July 1996: 20–22.

Marshall, Steve. "Hortense Packs a Punch, but USA Might be Spared." *USA Today*. 12 September 1996: A3.

Marshall, Tim. "A Passion for Prediction: There's More To Chasing Than Intercepting a Tornado." *Weatherwise*. April/May 1993: 22–26.

Mayfield, Max and Miles Lawrence. "Atlantic Hurricanes." *Weatherwise*. February/March 1996: 34–41.

McDonald, Kim A. "Preserving a Priceless Library of Ice." *The Chronicle of Higher Education*. 2 August 1996: A7+.

McDonald, Kim A. "Tornado-Chasing Scientists Use New Techniques to Probe the Origins of the Deadly Storms." *The Chronicle of Higher Education*. 12 July 1996: A9+.

McDonald, Kim A. "Unearthing Earth's Ancient Atmosphere Beneath Two Miles of Greenland Ice." *The Chronicle of Higher Education*. 2 August 1996: A6+.

Meredith, Robyn. "In Ohio River Valley, the Water's Edge Is Now It's Middle." *The New York Times*. 6 March 1997: A14.

Mervis, Jeffrey. "Agencies Scramble to Measure Public Impact of Research." *Science*. 5 July 1996: 27–28.

Mogil, H. Michael and Barbara G. Levine. "Gallery of Weather Pages." *Weatherwise*. August/September 1995: 15–16.

National Oceanic and Atmospheric Administration. *Are You Ready for a Winter Storm?* Washington: NOAA, 1991.

National Oceanic and Atmospheric Administration. *Heat Wave*. Washington: NOAA, 1994.

Nielsen, Clifford H. "Hurd Willett: Forecaster Extraordinaire." *Weatherwise*. August/September 1993: 38–44.

Pettengill, Steve. "Sailing by Satellite." *Weatherwise*. October/November 1995: 17–22.

Rice, Doyle. "Olympics: Gold Medal Forecasts." *Weatherwise*. June/July 1996: 10–12.

Richards, Steven J. "Hail To the Bronx: Using Weather To Turn City Kids On To Science." *Weatherwise*. August/September 1992: 24–28.

Rosenfeld, Jeff. "Cars vs. the Weather: A Century of Progress." *Weatherwise*. October/November 1996: 14–23.

Rosenfeld, Jeff. "Excitement in the Air." *Weatherwise*. June/July 1995: 71–72.

Rosenfeld, Jeff. "The Forgotten Hurricane." *Weatherwise*. August/September 1993: 13–18.

Rosenfeld, Jeff. "The Jumbo Outbreak." *Weatherwise*. June/July 1995: 58–59.

Rosenfeld, Jeff. "Spin Doctor: Talking Tornadoes with Howard Bluestein." *Weatherwise*. April/May 1996: 19–25.

Ryan, Bob. "A Window on Science: Watching the Weather Brings Out the Scientist In Everyone." *Weatherwise*. August/September 1993: 32–34.

Sack, Kevin. "Storm's Rains Bring Flooding in Two States." *The New York Times*. 8 September 1996: 1, 36.

Salopek, Paul. "Energy Dream Is Blowing In Midwest: Price Is Right, and Resource Is Unlimited." *The Chicago Tribune*. 6 February 1997: 1.

Schlatter, Thomas. "Weather Queries: Anatomy of a Heat Burst." *Weatherwise*. August/September 1995: 42–43.

Schlatter, Thomas. "Weather Queries: Dark Rays." *Weatherwise*. June/July 1996: 35–36.

Schlatter, Thomas. "Weather Queries: Snowrollers." *Weatherwise*. December 1996/January 1997: 42.

Shacham, Mordechai. "Danger by the Numbers: Meaningful Cold Weather Indicators." *Weatherwise*. October/November 1995: 27–28.

Shibley, John. "Glows Bands & Curtains." *Astronomy*. April 1995: 76–81.

Stevens, William K. "'95 Is Hottest Year on Record As the Global Trend Resumes." *The New York Times*. 4 January 1996: A1+.

"Stormy Weather Is On the Rise, Researchers Say Number of Blizzards, Rainstorms Jumps 20% in the U.S. Since 1900." *The Chicago Tribune*. 23 January 1997: 8.

Suplee, Curt. "Climatology: Carbon Dioxide Signals Change." *The Washington Post*. 23 September 1996: A2.

U.S. Department of Commerce. *Flash Floods*. Washington D.C.: U.S. Government Printing Office, 1982.

U.S. Department of Commerce. *Flash Floods and Floods. . . The Awesome Power!* Washington D.C.: NOAA, 1992.

U.S. Department of Commerce. *Heat Wave: A Major Summer Killer*. Washington D.C.: NOAA.

U.S. Department of Commerce. *Hurricanes. . . The Greatest Storms on Earth*. Washington D.C.: NOAA, 1994.

U.S. Department of Commerce. *NOAA Weather Radio*. Washington D.C.: NOAA, 1995.

U.S. Department of Commerce. *Thunderstorms and Lightning. . . The Underrated Killers!* Washington D.C.: NOAA, 1994.

U.S. Department of Commerce. *Tornado Safety Rules in Schools*. Washington D.C.: NOAA, 1981.

U.S. Department of Commerce. *Tornadoes. . . Nature's Most Violent Storms*. Washington D.C.: NOAA, 1992.

U.S. Department of Commerce. *Watch Out. . . Storms Ahead! Owlie Skywarn's Weather Book*. Washington D.C.: NOAA, 1984.

U.S. Department of Commerce. *Winter Storms: Terms to Know/How to Survive*. Washington D.C.: NOAA, 1982.

"Volunteers Pouring In to Assist Communities Ravaged by Floods." *The Los Angeles Times*. 11 March 1997: A13.

Wallace, John M. and Shawna Vogel. "El Niño and Climate Prediction." *Reports to the Nation on Our Changing Planet*. Washington D.C.: NOAA, Spring 1994.

Walsh, Edward. "Unpredictable Nature Inundates Many Towns: Flooding Hits Some Hard, Spares Others." *The Washington Post*. 7 March 1997: A3.

Walsh, Edward. "With Flood Waters At Their Door, A Few Stubborn Souls Ride It Out." *The Washington Post*. 8 March 1997: A3.

Wiche, Sandra. "Year of Extremes." *Weatherwise*. October/November 1995: 30–34.

Williams, Jack. "The Making of the Weather Page." *Weatherwise*. August/September 1992: 12–18.

Williams, Jack. "Watching the Vapor Channel: Satellites Put Forecasters On the Trail of Weather's Hidden Ingredient." *Weatherwise*. August/September 1993: 26–30.

Williams, Richard. "The Mystery of Disappearing Heat." *Weatherwise*. August/September 1996: 28–29.

WEBSITES

Note: the following website addresses are subject to change

Anyanwu, Azunna E. O. End-to-End Forecast Process and Event-Driven Versus Schedule-Driven Products. [Online] Available http://www.nws.noaa.gov/om/etoefp.htm, November 21, 1996.

Sources

Babel Fish Corporation. Chinook Winds. *The Alberta Traveller.* [Online] Available http:www.babelfish.com/AB_Travel/weather_guides/chinook.html, January 28, 1997.

Boulder Wind Info. [Online] Available http://cdc.noaa.gov/~cas/wind.html, January 28, 1997.

Dept. of Atmospheric Sciences, Univ. of Illinois at Urbana-Champaign. Cloud Catalog. [Online] Available http://covis.atmos.uiuc.edu/guide/clouds/html/cloud.home.html, January 9, 1997.

The GOES Project. [Online] Available http://climate.gsfc.nasa.gov/~chesters/goesproject.html, November 5, 1996.

High-Resolution Weather Forecasting Readied for Olympics. *Science & Engineering News.* [Online] Available http://ike.engr.washington.edu/news/bulletin/weather.html, November 21, 1996.

Janice Huff. *INTELLiCast biographies.* [Online] Available http://www.intellicast.com/weather/bio/wnbc/jh/bio.html, November 25, 1996.

MacDonald, Michael. WeatherNet. [Online] Available http://cirrus.sprl.umich.edu/wxnet/, September 10, 1996.

National Climatic Data Center. Billion Dollar U.S. Weather Disasters, 1980–1996. [Online] Available http://www.ncdc.noaa.gov/, November 19, 1996.

National Oceanic and Atmospheric Administration. [Online] Available http://www.noaa.gov/, November 19, 1996.

National Research Council. New Radar System Aids Weather Forecasting Nationwide but May Provide Less Radar Coverage for Some Areas. [Online] Available http://xerxes.nas.edu/onpi/pr/radar/, November 6, 1996.

NEXRAD NOW. [Online] Available http://www.osf.uoknor.edu/news/vol1is1.htm, November 6, 1996.

NOAA's Geostationary and Polar-Orbiting Weather Satellites. [Online] Available http://140.90.207.25:8080/EBB/ml/genlsatl.html, November 7, 1996.

Noel, James J. More Heavy Rain Has Hit Southern Indiana and Kentucky. [Online] Available http://www.nws.noaa.gov/er/iln/afos/CRWHMDCIN, March 18, 1997.

Null, Jan. NWS Glossary. [Online] Available http://www.nws.mbay.net:80/guide.html, January 29, 1997.

Palmer, Chad. Three Roads Will Improve Forecasts. *USA Today Weather.* [Online] Available http://www.usatoday.com/weather/wforkey.htm, November 21, 1996.

Plymouth State College, New Hampshire. PSC Meteorology Program Cloud Boutique. [Online] Available http://vortex.plymouth.edu/cloud.html, January 9, 1997.

S. California Winds May Fan Wildfires. *The Salt Lake Tribune.* [Online] Available http://www.sltrib.com:80/96/OCT/25/twr/00411040.htm, January 29, 1997.

San Diego NWS. Santa Ana Winds. [Online] Available http://nimbo.wrh.noaa.gov:80/Sandiego/snawind.html, January 29, 1997.

Songer, Nancy Butler. Global Exchange Weather Program. *Kids as Global Scientists.* [Online] Available http://www-kgs.colorado.edu/index.html, November 5, 1996.

Storm Chaser Homepage. [Online] Available http://taiga.geog.niu.edu/chaser/chaser.html, November 18, 1996.

Tornado Outbreak, Flood Index. *USA Today Weather.* [Online] Available http://www.usatoday.com/weather/wlead.htm, March 18, 1997.

The Tornado Project Online. [Online] Available http://www.tornadoproject.com, November 18, 1996.

USA Today Weather. [Online] Available http://www.usatoday.com/weather/wfront. htm, November 18, 1996.

The Weather Channel. [Online] Available http://www.weather.com/, September 19, 1996.

Weather Underground. [Online] Available http://www.wunderground.com/, September 10, 1996.

WeatherNet: WeatherSites. [Online] Available http://cirrus.sprl.umich.edu/ wxnet/servers.html, September 10, 1996.

Women in Weather. . . Mini-Biographies. [Online] Available http://www.nssl. uoknor.edu/~nws/women/biograph.html, September 10, 1996.

WX-ACCESS One: World Wide Web Amateur Weather Connection. *American*

Weather Observer. [Online] Available http://members.aol.com/larrypahl/awo. htm, November 18, 1996.

CD-ROMs

Eyewitness Encyclopedia of Science. New York: Dorling Kindersley, Inc., 1994.

McGraw-Hill Multimedia Encyclopedia of Science and Technology. New York: McGraw-Hill, Inc., 1996.

The 1996 Grolier Multimedia Encyclopedia. Danbury, CT: Grolier Electronic Publishing, Inc., 1996.

Science Navigator. New York: McGraw-Hill, Inc., 1995.

Science On File CD-ROM. New York: Facts on File, Inc., 1995.

Index

Italic type indicates volume number;
(ill.) indicates illustration (photographs and figures).

A

Absolute humidity *1:* 46, 48-50

Absolute zero *1:* 6

Accretion *2:* 207

AccuWeather *3:* 439

Acid fog *3:* 513

Acid rain *3:* 486, 500, 512-513, 513 (ill.), 515

Acid rain experiment *3:* 515

Adiabatic processes *1:* 55

Adjustment to sea level *3:* 449-450

Advection fog *1:* 54, 112-113, 113 (ill.)

Aerogenerators *3:* 519

Aerologists *3:* 410

Agassiz, Jean Louis *3:* 480-482, 480 (ill.)

Agricultural reports *3:* 437-438, 443

Air-mass thunderstorm *2:* 218-219

Air-mass weather *1:* 34

Air masses *1:* 18; *2:* 266; *3:* 406

Air parcels *1:* 48; *2:* 212

Air pollutants *3:* 507-511, 513

Air pollution *3:* 500, 506-511, 507 (ill.), 509 (ill.)

Air pressure *1:* 13, 16, 18, 102; *3:* 422, 425, 392 (ill.), 393

Air stability. *See* Stable air layers *and* Unstable air layers

Albedo *3:* 482

Alberta Clippers *2:* 200

Alphabetical list of local winds *1:* 121

Alternative transportation *3:* 517, 518 (ill.)

Altocumulus clouds *1:* 81-82, 81 (ill.), 82 (ill.), 86, 92, 96, 99, 105, 107-108; *2:* 190

Altocumulus castellanus clouds *1:* 105, 105 (ill.)

Altocumulus undulatus clouds *1:* 96

C

Italic type indicates volume number; (ill.) indicates illustration (photographs and figures).

Coronas *2:* 334, 335 (ill.)

Coronas *2:* 334, 335 (ill.)
Coxwell, Robert *1:* 14, 14 (ill.)
Crepuscular rays *2:* 320, 320 (ill.)
Critical angle *2:* 332
Cumuliform clouds *1:* 75, 88, 99, 106; *2:* 185-186, 198-199
Cumulonimbus clouds *1:* 39, 88-89, 90 (ill.), 92, 98-99, 107, 108; *2:* 182-183, 195, 207, 211, 214-215, 219, 229, 231, 266
Cumulonimbus calvus clouds *1:* 93
Cumulonimbus incus clouds *1:* 90, 105
Cumulonimbus mammatus clouds *1:* 99, 99 (ill.)
Cumulus clouds *1:* 82, 83, 87 (ill.), 88, 92; *2:* 182-183, 191, 212, 214-215, 219, 221, 229, 267
Cumulus congestus clouds *1:* 89, 98-99; *2:* 258
Cumulus humilis clouds *1:* 97, 98 (ill.), 105
Cumulus mediocris clouds *1:* 89, 89 (ill.), 98
Cumulus stage *2:* 214-215
Cup anemometers *3:* 396, 399 (ill.)
Cyclogenesis *1:* 42, 43 (ill.)
Cyclones *1:* 28, 33, 41, 127; *2:* 243, 264

D

Dalton, John *1:* 15, 15 (ill.)
Dart leaders *2:* 233
De Coriolis, Gustave-Gaspard *1:* 20, 20 (ill.)
De Bort, Teisserenc *1:* 14
Decay stage *2:* 250
Deforestation *3:* 486, 502 (ill.)
Dehydration *2:* 297
Dendrites *2:* 196-197
Dendrochronology *3:* 498
Deposition *1:* 52, 62; *2:* 195, 198
Deposition nuclei *1:* 63
Derechos *1:* 122, 138, 140 (ill.); *2:* 211, 226, 237
Desert climates *3:* 454, 460-462
Desert pavement *1:* 143
Deserts *3:* 451, 460-462, 462 (ill.)
Destructive interference *2:* 334
Developing stage *2:* 214
Dew *1:* 50, 50 (ill.); *2:* 181
Dew and fog experiment *1:* 55
Dew point *1:* 15, 18, 49, 54-55, 58-59, 69, 75, 79, 81, 92, 109-110, 114, 117; *2:* 212, 214, 244; *3:* 392, 424, 464, 478
Dew-point temperature *3:* 389 (ill.)
Diamond dust *1:* 119

Italic type indicates volume number; (ill.) indicates illustration (photographs and figures).

F

Italic type indicates volume number; (ill.) indicates illustration (photographs and figures).

G

H

Italic type indicates volume number; (ill.) indicates illustration (photographs and figures).

L

Lake breezes *1:* 124
Lake-effect snow *2:* 200, 201 (ill.)
Land breeze experiment *1:* 68
Land breezes *1:* 67, 113, 123, 123 (ill.), 140
Latent heat *1:* 7, 42, 51, 57-58, 67; *2:* 191, 217, 231, 259, 268; *3:* 390
Lavoisier, Antoine-Laurent *1:* 11, 11 (ill.)
Leeward slopes *1:* 69, 101-102, 127-128, 130, 142; *3:* 453, 478
Lenticular clouds *1:* 100, 100 (ill.)
Lestes *1:* 122, 134
Levanters *1:* 122, 141
Leveches *1:* 122, 134
Light, color of. *See* Color of light
Light, scattering of. *See* Scattering of light
Lightning *2:* 211, 215, 226, 229, 230 (ill.), 232-236, 243, 248
Lightning rods *2:* 229, 236, 236 (ill.)
Lightning safety *2:* 227
Little Ice Age *3:* 485-486, 494
Local winds *1:* 121-149
Lorenz, Edward *3:* 376, 377 (ill.), 444

M

Macrobursts *2:* 226, 237
Major cloud groups *1:* 77 (ill.)
Major El Niño event *1:* 73
Mammatus clouds *1:* 99; *2:* 222
Marine climates *3:* 455, 464-466
Marine forecasts *3:* 443, 445
Marine reports *3:* 438
Maritime tropical air mass *2:* 219
Mature stage *2:* 214-215, 217, 229, 231, 249
Maunder, E. W., *3:* 494
Maunder minimum *3:* 494
Maximum and minimum thermometers *3:* 385 (ill.), 386-387, 405
Measuring atmospheric conditions *3:* 385
Measuring climate change *3:* 494
Media weathercasting *3:* 431
Mediterranean climates *3:* 455, 464, 466-467, 466 (ill.)
Melting zone *2:* 189
Meltwater equivalent *3:* 398-399
Mercury barometers *3:* 393-394, 393 (ill.)
Mesocyclones *2:* 226, 248-249
Mesoscale convective complex *2:* 220

Italic type indicates volume number; (ill.) indicates illustration (photographs and figures).

Nitric acid *3:* 512
Nitric oxide *3:* 511
Nitrogen dioxide *3:* 511-512
Nitrogen oxides *3:* 511
NOAA Weather Radio *3:* 437-438
NOAA-K satellites *3:* 419
Non-tornadic waterspouts *2:* 257
Nor'easter *1:* 122, 137
Northeaster *1:* 137
Northern temperate climates *3:* 455, 467-469, 468 (ill.), 476-477
Nor'wester *1:* 122, 130

O

Obliquity *3:* 490
Occluded fronts *1:* 40, 40 (ill.), 44
Ocean currents *1:* 22, 70, 71 (ill.); *3:* 451, 488
Ocean and lake sediments *3:* 497
Oceanographic satellites *3:* 419
Optical effects *2:* 317-338
Organized convection theory *2:* 270
Organizing stage *2:* 249
Orographic clouds *1:* 100
Orographic lifting *1:* 61, 68; *3:* 453
Orographic thunderstorms *2:* 219
Overshooting *2:* 222
Ozone depletion *3:* 500, 513-516
Ozone hole *3:* 514
Ozone layer *1:* 4, 11, 13; *3:* 514-516

P

Paleoclimatologists *3:* 494
Paleozoic Era *3:* 479, 482
Pamperos *1:* 122, 138
Pangea *3:* 482
Papagayos *1:* 122, 126
Paper hygrometer experiment *3:* 390-391
Particulate matter *3:* 509-510
Pascal, Blaise *1:* 17, 17 (ill.)
Permafrost *3:* 470, 472
Phase changes *1:* 7
Phased array antennas *3:* 415
Photochemical smog *3:* 509 (ill.)

Italic type indicates volume number; (ill.) indicates illustration (photographs and figures).

Italic type indicates volume number; (ill.) indicates illustration (photographs and figures).

T

Italic type indicates volume number; (ill.) indicates illustration (photographs and figures).

Index

Unskilled forecasts *3:* 370-371
Unstable air layers *1:* 59, 59 (ill.), 83; *2:* 212, 220
Unstable atmosphere. *See* Unstable air layers
Updrafts *2:* 183, 186, 207, 216, 218, 221-222, 225-226, 248, 259
Upper-air westerlies *1:* 26, 29, 29 (ill.), 31; *2:* 224, 292
Upslope fog *1:* 116 (ill.), 117
Upwelling *1:* 71-72; *3:* 451, 466
U.S. Weather Bureau *2:* 281

V

Valley breezes *1:* 124
Valley fog *1:* 111, 112 (ill.), 119
Vapor channel *3:* 417
Vapor pressure *1:* 64; *2:* 197
Veering winds *3:* 381
Ventifacts *1:* 145
Vernal equinoxes *1:* 2
Vertical clouds *1:* 124
Virga *1:* 86, 105; *2:* 185, 186 (ill.), 200, 237; *3:* 460
Visible radiation *3:* 416-417
Volatile organic compounds (VOCs), *3:* 511
Volcanoes *3:* 486, 490-492, 492 (ill.)
Von Helmholtz, Hermann *1:* 103
Vonnegut, Bernard *2:* 190
Vortexes *2:* 243

W

Wall clouds *2:* 255
Warm clouds *1:* 66; *2:* 182
Warm fronts *1:* 37, 85-86, 105-108, 115, 117; *2:* 220
Water cycles *1:* 66; *2:* 190
Water mirages *2:* 325
Waterspouts *2:* 255, 257-261
Weather aircraft *2:* 288; *3:* 410-412, 411 (ill.)
Weather balloons *3:* 409
Weather Central *3:* 439
The Weather Channel *3:* 432
Weather forecasts *3:* 422-427, 441-442
Weather instrument resources *3:* 383-384
Weather log *3:* 402
Weather maps *3:* 428-430, 431 (ill.)
Weather modification *2:* 190

Italic type indicates volume number; (ill.) indicates illustration (photographs and figures).